MW01713244

BACKACHE

PREVENTION AND CURE

By

Dr. Dhiren Gala

B.Sc., D.H.M.S., D.O., D.Ac.,
C.G.O., C.C.H., A.R.S.H.

Recipient of a gold medal for extraordinary work in the field of Alternative Therapeutics

With

Dr. D. R. Gala
N.D., D.N.O., D.C.O.

Dr. Sanjay Gala
M.B. (BOM.), M.S. (ENT)

NAVNEET®

NAVNEET PUBLICATIONS (INDIA) LIMITED

Navneet House, Gurukul Road, Memnagar, Ahmadabad – 380 052. Phone : 6630 5000

Navneet Bhavan, B. S. Road, Dadar, Mumbai – 400 028. Phone : 6662 6565

DHANLAL BROTHERS DISTRIBUTORS

70, Princess Street, Mumbai – 400 002.
Phone : 2201 7027/2205 3716

G 4518

Visit us at : www.navneet.com | **e-mail :** npil@navneet.com

Price : Rs. 57.00

Dr. Dhiren Gala

1st Floor, Abbas Building 'A',
Near Tilak Market, Jalbhai Lane,
Harkishandas Hospital Road,
Mumbai – 400 004.

Phone : 2386 7275

Published by Navneet Publications (India) Ltd., Dantali, Gujarat.
Printed by Navneet Publications (India) Ltd., Dantali, Gujarat.

[24–4–08 (14) : 3]

PREFACE

Almost eight persons out of ten suffer from acute backache at least once in their lives. About sixty percent of backache sufferers belong to the age group of 21-40 years. In other words, backache strikes persons when they are in the prime of their lives. Gloomy statistics, indeed.

Backache is a major cause of absenteeism in industry. The resultant loss of production makes industrialists lose their sleep. If the industry is concerned about the waste of money, we are just as concerned about the waste of people. Sincere and hard-working, they don't want to cause any difficulty and yet, because of back problems, they are unable to perform their jobs effectively.

Each day, thousands (perhaps lakhs) of persons remain absent from work and cannot fulfil social responsibilities because of backache. Thus, back pain is a major social problem. What cannot be expressed in numbers, although it is of equal or greater importance, is the profound suffering and compromise in the quality of life that backache victims experience.

We believe that a doctor must fully enlighten and educate the patient about his or her backache. A doctor must not only tell what is wrong but what the diagnosis means, what it can develop into and why certain treatment is prescribed. Unfortunately, there are not many doctors who have the time or the inclination for such discussion with their patients. That is one reason for bringing out this book.

However, the more important reason for the publication of this book is the realisation on our part that back-care should be directed more at prevention of backache rather than its treatment. Prevention is better than cure. And backache is a disorder that is easy to prevent.

We have tried to remain clear and simple; but, we have not withheld important concepts and facts about back-care just because they seem technical or complex. We believe that an exposure to all relevant information on this subject will be to the reader's benefit.

Finally, the information given in this book is based not only on our own experience but has also been drawn from that of some world-authorities in the field of back-care. That is to say, the reader is not just getting a 'one man's opinion'; there is a lot of scientific evidence to back the information offered.

Suggestions for the improvement of this book will not only be gratefully acknowledged and but will also be considered while bringing out its future editions.

– Authors

CONTENTS

1. INTRODUCTION

What does back trouble mean to you ?

* Constant misery ?
* An unforgettable and painful week ?
* A stiff and painful back in the morning ?
* An odd twinge in the back ?
* Something that happens to somebody else ?

Try listing the names of ten adult friends at random. If eight of them are backache victims and only two have managed to remain free from this trouble, they are a set of typical persons. If you are one of the eight unfortunates (and the fact you are opening this book means you probably are), the problem becomes acutely personal in terms of pain and inconvenience.

You may not, so far, have experienced it yourself, especially if you are young and fit. But are you immune to backache ? The answer is a most emphatic 'no'.

Even if you have not suffered from any back problem so far, the chances are that you may do so in near future unless, of course, you take appropriate preventive measures without delay. That is a prediction based on the statistical data available.

Perhaps with the exception of headache, back pain, particularly in the lower or lumbar region of the spine, is the most common scourges of mankind. Very few people live their lives without experiencing backache in one form or another. It may be just a temporary inconvenience that comes and goes; or it could interfere continuously and relentlessly with work, rest and sleep. In other words, backaches are so common that it is fair to say that most people suffer from several acute short attacks and one or two longer-lasting ones in their lifetime. However, only a minority of these attacks are due to a serious disease; but all are extremely tedious, preventing the leading of a normal life and restricting work, hobbies and the enjoyment of life for weeks, months and sometimes even years. People visit doctors for backache more often than for any other ailment, except respiratory infections (especially cold, cough and flu). More varieties of over-the-counter pills, liniments and other medications are sold for relief of backache than for any other problem, including headaches and the common cold. Many a person with backache have come to accept a drug-dominated life.

If you have a statistical bent of mind, here are some figures :

Epidemiological studies reveal that back pain afflicts a staggering sixty to eighty per cent of the population. The figures are higher in the developed western countries than in the developing countries. The more automated a society is, the higher is the incidence of back problems. Back problems occur more commonly

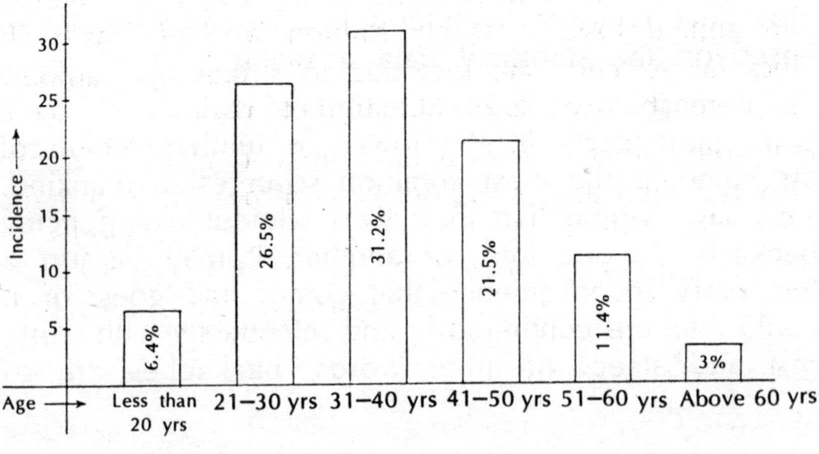

in persons between the age-groups of 21 to 40. However, no age-group is exempt as the graph on page 6 indicates.

It is clear from the graph that there is a high incidence of back problems in people who are in the prime of life, i.e., who are aged between 21 to 40 years. The belief that backache is a degenerative disorder affecting only the elderly persons is a myth. In reality, back pain is a major, and basically unappreciated, problem for young adults and the middle-aged. In fact, back problems tend to somewhat lessen as we get older. Nature has seen to it that our backs, like fine wine, get better with age !

The incidence of backache is almost the same for both sexes. However, women are more susceptible during pregnancy. The cause for this has been discussed at length in chapter 11.

Backaches cause more off-work occasions than most diseases. Back pain is the second leading cause of absenteeism in industry after the common cold. Corresponding figures for our country are not available but in Britain, back pain compels more than 50,000 persons to take leave from work everyday, causing an annual loss of twenty million working days. This loss far exceeds the loss due to strikes and amounts to a terrible waste of human potential.

Well, that sounds a bit grim and gloomy, doesn't it ? But then that is the outcome of our total ignorance regarding the structure of our back, how it works and why it responds in certain ways. Our apathy towards the matter of our own health also contributes to this state of affairs. Indeed, most doctors, too, reach their wit's end when asked to advise about the prevention of back disorders. Conferences, symposia and workshops are organized to educate patients or doctors in the prevention and the management of disorders like diabetes, high blood pressure, obesity, ischemic heart disease or AIDS. But conferences dedicated to the cause of back-welfare have not been heard off; indeed, a matter of shame.

This ignorance on the part of patients is evident while listening to their explanation for the probable cause of their backache.

"Its natural; I am getting older."

"I have been working too hard and something had to give in – it was my back."

"I have got a slipped disc."

"I lifted a water-bucket the wrong way and it injured my back."

"Weak backs run in my family."

"My back aches because my bed is too soft."

Not one of our patients has ever told us : "My back is aching because my back muscles are weak and I have poor posture." In fact, we don't even expect them to offer this explanation. People have never been enlightened or educated about how the back functions nor has it been explained to them why strong muscles and good posture will help prevent backache.

The purpose of this book, then, is fourfold : (1) to demonstrate how poor posture and weak muscles contribute to common low backache; (2) to offer simple tests with the help of which you can judge the fitness of your back; (3) to show you simple exercises that will help prevent backache for the rest of your life; (4) to show you how to use your back more effectively in your day-to-day activities.

This book will also tell you about the other much less common causes of backache, and how to cope with an acute attack of back pain. Armed with this knowledge, you will be able to live without perpetual fear and discomfort.

The book also discusses various aspects of the treatment of chronic back pain. Just because you have had a bad attack of back pain, don't think you are going to be paralysed, or crippled or severely incapacitated – this just isn't true. Backache, however chronic, can be effectively treated – and then prevented from recurring.

The succeeding chapters will enlighten you about all the aspects of back problems and, especially, about how to prevent backache by strengthening the key postural muscles. So read on.

2. BACK : ITS STRUCTURE AND FUNCTION

The back is the plodding work-horse of our body, ignored while it steadily and relentlessly does its job. We care little for, and hence don't know much about, our back : what is its structure like and how does it work.

When, while conversing with you, your doctor refers to anatomical structures, does it seem to your ears as if he is speaking of some distant galaxies or exotic topographical points ? That is what happens when a lay person is confronted with anatomical terminology.

You may think anatomy too complicated, boring or scary to contemplate it in any depth. But philosophers and scientists have always extolled the beauty of human anatomy and we happen to agree with them. We would strongly urge you to interest yourself particularly in the structure of your back. That will help you to interpret your doctor's conversation easily (albeit, you should feel free to ask him to explain things in plain English). Besides, we believe that an informed patient is a co-operative and relaxed patient. A person who takes active interest in his or her own health by procuring the knowledge about how the back works and why it acts and reacts in certain ways, actually speeds up his or her own recovery.

Let us, then, consider the back and its components i.e., the spinal cord, the backbone, the muscles and the ligaments.

First of all, let's be clear as to what we mean by the spinal cord. This is not, as people often think, a part of the spine or the backbone. As you can see from fig. 2.1, it is actually a continuation of the brain – a column of nerve tissue that runs down from the base of the skull to the level of the small of the back.

What does the spinal cord do ? Well, basically it is a relayer of messages. The roots of various nerves run out from it; these nerves supply the arms, the legs, the internal organs and, in fact, all parts of the body.

When you decide to move, let us say, your leg, what happens is that your brain sends a message

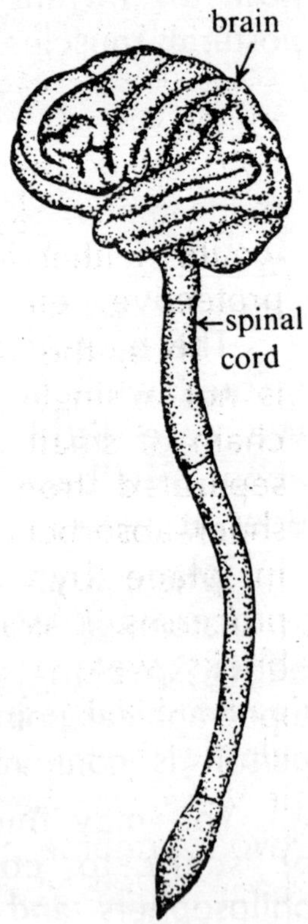

Fig. 2.1

down the spinal cord and into the nerves which lead to the muscles in the leg. When the latter get this signal, they move.

Messages travel in the opposite direction, too. If you happen to touch a hot utensil with your foot, pain signals travel up the nerves of the foot and then into the spinal cord, which carries them on up to the brain. Only when they arrive at the brain, are you consciously aware of the pain.

So the spinal cord is basically the great communications channel of the body. If it is damaged – which happens only at the time of a fairly severe injury–then there will be serious trouble. But happily, hardly any of the various disorders causing back pain produce damage to the spinal cord.

You must have, perhaps, realized that the spinal cord is a vitally important organ like the brain. You might suppose that the ideal way to shield the spinal cord would be with a straight, one-piece bony tube, much as the skull protects the brain. But such a spine would neither allow motion nor possess the necessary protective, energy-absorbing properties.

Thus, the backbone, as the name would suggest, is not a single bone but a column or a long vertical chain of small bony units called vertebrae, which are separated from one another by firm and resilient shock-absorbers called intervertebral discs and held in place by strong muscles, ligaments and bony processes. It is as though in a column, the constituent bricks were separated from one another by rubber pads instead of mortar and laced together by strong elastic thongs allowing the brick column to wave, as it were, in the breeze. The movement between any two vertebrae is quite small. But since there is a large number of vertebrae, considerable movement, indeed, is possible at the spine.

A visit to the natural history section of a museum will show you the various varieties of spines in different animals, birds, reptiles and fishes ranging from the giant dinosaurs and whales to the smallest of birds and fishes. The pattern of the backbone is similar in all species and it serves the same purposes, viz,

(1) to house and protect the spinal cord, the vital cable linking the brain to all other parts of the body,

(2) to bear the arms (through the shoulder girdle), the legs (through the pelvic girdle), the skull and the ribs,

(3) to provide broad, bony areas for the attachment of muscles, ligaments and tendons that permit the body's movement.

Our spine is a compromise between two opposite necessities : that of stability and that of mobility.

The tall column of bone must be cohesive enough to maintain its essential shape, even while bearing a heavy weight. It must also withstand both vertical and horizontal stresses. If the various vertebrae were hinged together as loosely as our elbows or knees so that each pair of vertebrae could flop back and forth over a 90 degree angle, we would, perhaps, not be able even to rise to a sitting posture. We would certainly be unable to stand up and walk.

The requirement of stability could be met by making the spine a single rigid piece of bone. But that would either make most of our familiar movements impossible or would grossly curtail them. Flexibility is the second necessity.

Happily, our spine, through its peculiar structure, efficiently integrates these two opposing properties of stability and mobility. That makes it one of the most fascinating and elegant of all mechanical structures in the animal kingdom, indeed, a marvel of biological engineering.

All animals, except human beings, are quadrupeds. In man's evolution, the spine has had to modify its function considerably through the ages, for his remote ancestors swung from bough to bough, and only took to an erect posture and erect walking relatively late during the evolutionary process. The smart soldier, shoulders drawn back, chest blown forward and standing to attention as stiff and straight as a ramrod may make an impressive figure. But it is the most unnatural one in terms of spinal evolution. In a recent television programme featuring dogs, the show was stolen by a poodle walking erect on its hind legs – a highly impressive feat but unnatural. We can only hope that the poor beast has not since developed a backache !

We have drifted away somewhat from the topic of this chapter. Let us again come back to the structure of the spine.

The spinal column comprises of 33 small and generally flat bones called vertebrae, sitting one on top of the other from the neck to the top of the buttocks. As you can see in figure 2.2, the vertebral column has a double 's' shape. It curves slightly forwards in the neck, slightly backward in the chest, slightly forward again in the small of the back and backward again in its lowest part. For simplification, doctors divide the spine into five regions :

(1) The cervical region : This is the neck area of the spine comprising of seven upper vertebrae, the uppermost of which supports the head. The cervical spine, especially the joint between the first cervical vertebra and the skull, is very flexible so that you can move your head backwards and forwards, or from side to side, or turn it. We like to think of these cervical vertebrae as the 'yes' and 'no' bones because they allow us to nod 'yes' and shake our heads to express 'no'.

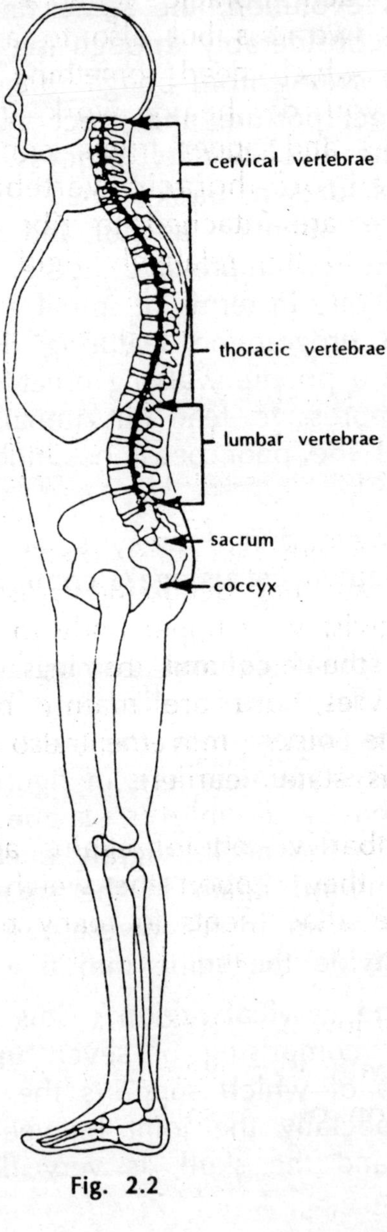

Fig. 2.2

(2) The thoracic (or dorsal) region : This is the backside of the chest area, comprising of twelve vertebrae. These vertebrae are larger and heavier than those of the cervical region. The reason for this is that each thoracic vertebra gives attachment not only to two ribs but also to a number of powerful muscles which need something firm to pull against. When you do heavy work involving your arms, shoulders and upper trunk, considerable stresses are produced on thoracic vertebrae. Since thoracic vertebrae are attached to ribs, which, in turn, are attached to the relatively rigid sternum (the vertical breast-bone), only slight movement, in the form of rotation, occurs in this region of the spine.

(3) The lumbar region : This area, also called the small of the back, comprises of five vertebrae. Like the cervical spine, the lumbar spine, too, is very flexible allowing a variety of movements. Stand upright and bow from the waist; then lean backwards as far as you can; then bend sidewards as much as possible; finally, twist your upper body to the right and the left keeping the hips and the legs straight. In all these manoeuvres, you are mainly moving your lumbar spine (the twisting movement also occurs at the thoracic spine, as stated earlier).

Lumbar vertebrae, again, are large and strong because they support the weight of the upper body and give attachments to many powerful muscles that move the trunk and the legs.

Most low back pains originate because of something wrong with the muscles, ligaments or vertebrae of this region of the spine.

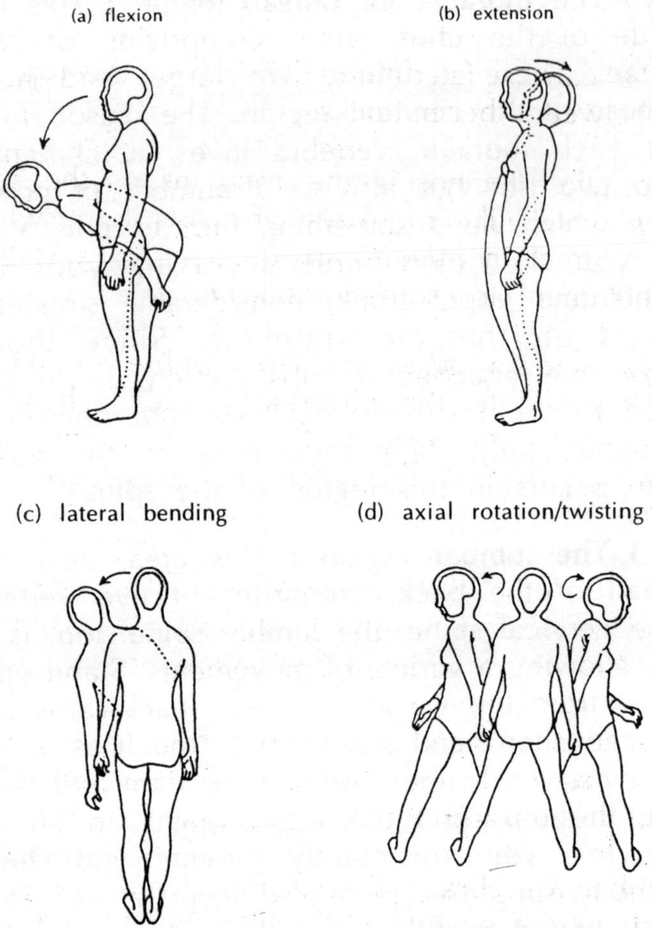

Fig. 2.3

(4) The sacral region : This is the area just above the buttocks. No significant movement is possible in this part of the spine because the five vertebrae that make it up are fused together to form a single, broad, triangular structure called the sacrum. The sacrum, on its sides, gives attachment to the two innominate (hip) bones. These three bones together form the pelvis – a cavity which protects important structures like the uterus, the bowel and the urinary bladder.

(5) The coccyx : This is the lowermost part of the spine formed by the fusion of four very small vertebrae. It can be felt under the skin at the top of the cleft between the buttocks.

In fact, the coccyx is the remnant of the tail found in primates like monkeys who use it to swing from tree to tree. In humans, it functions as a stable site of attachment for some muscles.

Coccyx seldom gives rise to trouble or pain. However, if you suffer the misfortune of falling heavily on your bottom (the sort of thing that happens if somebody plays the foolish trick of whipping your chair away when you were about to sit), you may injure this tail. Such coccygeal pain is known to persist for a long time, sometimes even months, though no fracture is usually seen on a radiograph (X-ray). Eventually, however, the pain does go away.

Let us now transfer our attention from generals to particulars, i.e., study the structure of a vertebra, the intervertebral disc and the key postural muscles.

A lumbar vertebra : Each lumbar vertebra is a strong and flat bone with a disc-like 'body' in front, a vertebral 'arch' (hole) just behind the body and a projection (spinous process) at the back.

The body of the vertebra is meant to bear the weight of the upper body. The vertebral arch lodges the spinal cord, which is thus protected. The back part of the vertebra has facet joints which are partly responsible for the movements of the trunk. Thus, a vertebra serves three functions : weight-bearing, movement and protection of the spinal cord.

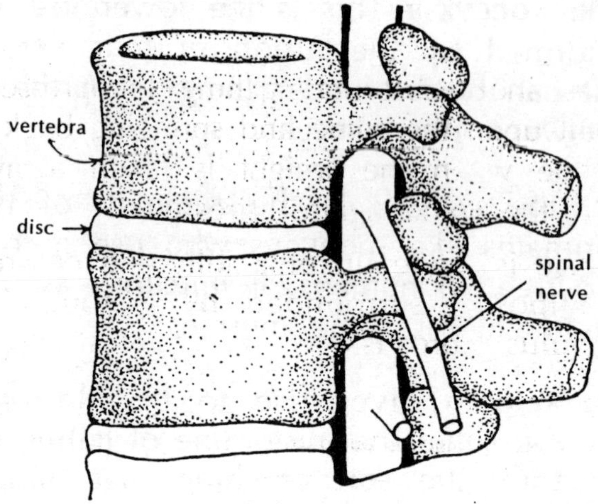

Lateral view

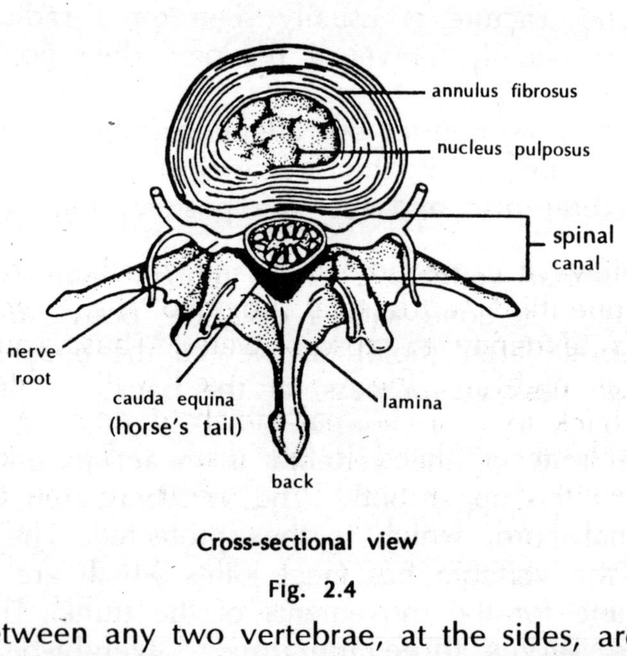

Cross-sectional view

Fig. 2.4

Between any two vertebrae, at the sides, are gaps (called intervertebral foramina) which allow spinal nerves to come out (see fig. 2.4).

The disc : Discs are very tough yet flexible structures or cushions of cartilage that separate any two vertebrae. They act as shock-absorbers getting compressed when weight is put upon the spine and springing back to their original shape when the weight is taken away. Thus, they protect the spine against stresses.

Each disc is made up of a jelly-like centre called 'nucleus pulposus' surrounded by a tough capsule called 'annulus fibrosus'.

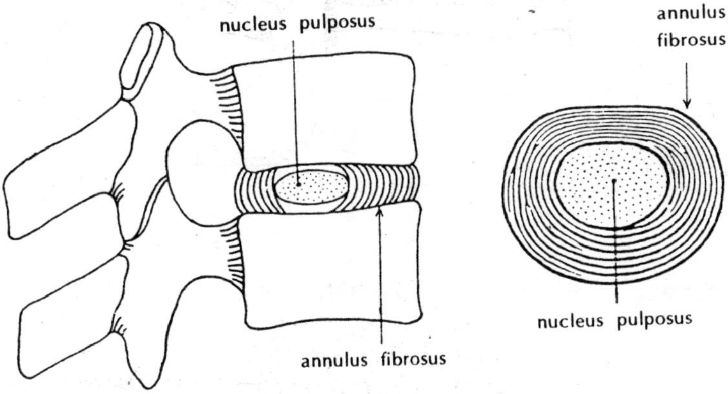

Fig. 2.5

Believe it or not, the discs, all together, constitute about one-third of the total length of the spine. They have a tendency to absorb water. Thus, you grow taller at night as the discs swell with water and shrink back to your 'normal' height during the day as the water accumulated in the discs is forced out (by the weight of the trunk). This swelling of the discs is even more marked in a weightless state, as astronauts may find out to their discomfiture. During a space flight, astronauts may actually grow as much as two inches taller, giving rise to back discomfort. Albeit, we need not worry about zero-gravity conditions, since there is little likehood of our travelling in a spaceship.

Because of the jelly-like soft centre and some amount of accumulated water, a disc acts as an efficient hydraulic system, dispersing pressure on the spine evenly in all directions along the back.

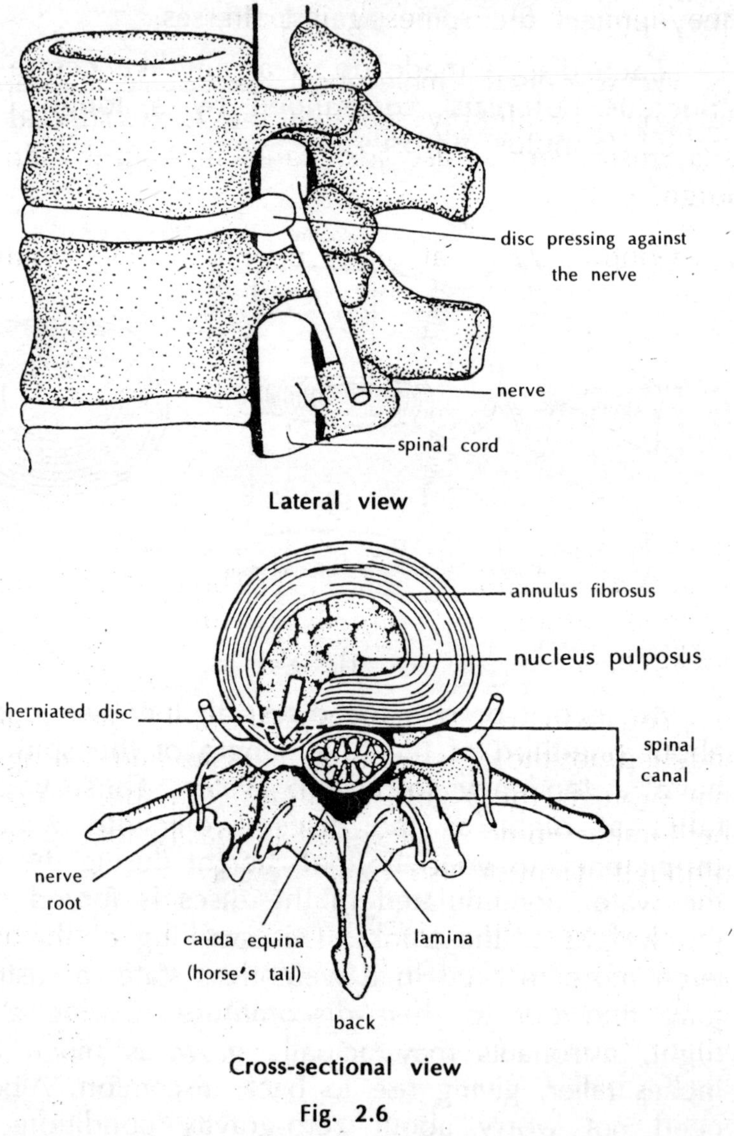

Fig. 2.6

The otherwise tough annulus fibrosus which forms the outer part of a disc is somewhat weak at the back and the sides of the disc. If it gives way or gets torn, it may allow the nucleus pulposus to bulge out. If this bulge presses against one of the spinal nerves (see figure 2.6) the result is pain.

We will discuss more about disc-trouble in chapter 3. But you can already see that the term 'slipped disc' is a misnomer; a disc just can't slip out—it can only bulge.

Contrary to what many people believe (thanks to doctors' propaganda), disc trouble isn't anywhere near the commonest cause of back pain. According to a number of authorities, disc trouble accounts for a mere five to seven per cent of all cases of low backache.

The working of the lower back : Let us now focus our attention on the five lumbar vertebrae as regards their working. These vertebrae are the trouble-makers, responsible, directly or indirectly, for most backaches.

You will recall that the thoracic vertebrae are attached to the ribs forming a rigid and strong cage that protects the heart and lungs. On the other hand, the lumbar spine is designed primarily for movement, although it must also bear weight.

However, these two functions, i.e., moving the trunk and bearing weight cannot be easily carried out at the same time. If such an activity is carried out which combines lumbar movements with lifting weight (e.g., a ballet dancer or a gymnast moving and holding a partner aloft), the lumbar region becomes susceptible or vulnerable to injury.

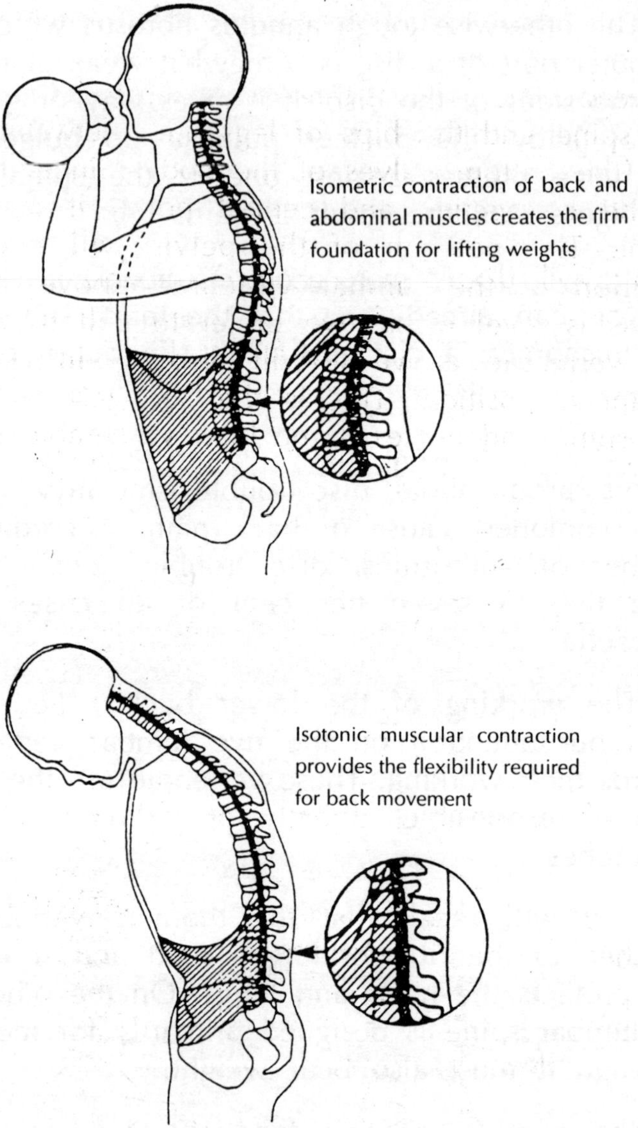

Fig. 2.7

Stacked one on top of another, the five lumbar vertebrae work as a unit, in a concerted manner, to permit forward bending, backward bending, etc. This working unit or column 'sits' on a firm foundation or a scaffolding called the pelvic platform. Our thighs bones, too, are attached to the sides of the pelvis. Therefore, the pelvis is the connecting structure between the spine and the hips of legs, i.e., between the top and the bottom halves of the body. Since the pelvis is the connecting and central point, it acts like a pivot. The position of the pelvis will control the position of the lumbar vertebrae above it. If the pelvis is level or, as we prefer to call it, balanced, the vertebrae above it will also be in a level or balanced position. This is the strongest position for the spine and makes it the least vulnerable to injury. However, if the pelvis is thrust forward, the vertebrae above it will curve out of alignment. Such out-of-alignment vertebrae cause wedging of the discs and potential discomfort to facet joints and make the spine weak and the back vulnerable to injury. On the other hand, when the lumbar vertebrae are aligned properly because the pelvis is in a balanced position, pressure is taken off the discs, the facet joints are unloaded and maximum space is provided for the exit of nerve roots.

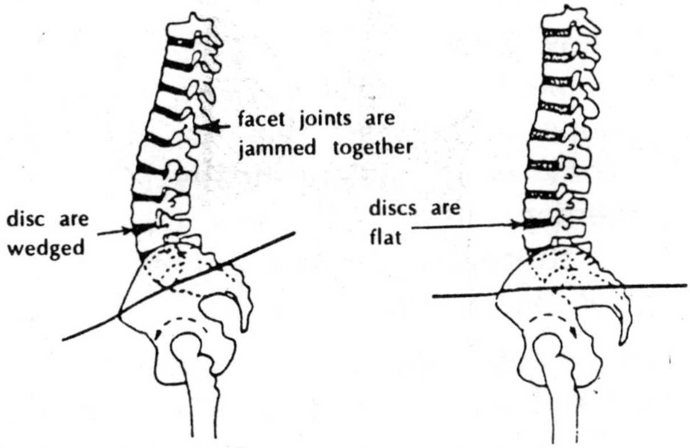

UNBALANCED PELVIS : weak position ; back is vulnerable to injury

BALANCED PELVIS : strongest position for the back

Fig. 2.8

This all-important 'pelvic balance' is a function of four groups of muscles. We shall learn more about these muscles soon.

The bones are the static, unchangeable part of the body. The muscles are the dynamic component, giving movement and life to the body. Back muscles play an important role in backache, as we shall see in chapter 3. They are controllable elements responding to the environment and controlled by our conscious thought processes. Composed of contractile fibres that are responsive to nerve-impulses, muscles comprise almost 40 per cent of our body weight and a large part of our body-bulk. There are some 140 muscles attached to the spine alone and they do a prodigious amount of work.

A muscle is basically a contractile tissue, i.e., it functions and carries out messages by contracting or shortening and relaxing or lengthening. The more a muscle is used or worked, the more it develops and gains in strength. If it is not used as much as it should be, it weakens and becomes flabby or loose. If it is not used at all, it atrophies or wastes away.

We are now going to discuss the specific muscles that are associated with and support the spine. There are four groups of muscles that are associated with the back. They work synergistically, that is to say they are interdependent and work together. All four groups are, therefore, important for the proper functioning of the back.

(1) The erector spinae (sacro-spinalis) muscles : These are the back muscles which hold the spine erect. If you place your entire palm flat against the middle of your lower back and walk, you will feel these muscles alternately contracting and relaxing. They provide posterior support for the back and have to work hard when you push or pull heavy weights, bend over, arch your back or hold your spine very erectly. These muscles can be quite painful when they get tensed and cramped up in spasms.

(2) The rectus abdominis muscles : People are often surprised when told that these abdominal muscles are extremely important for the back. These muscles, which appear like narrow vertical bands or straps on the front of the abdomen, provide support to the front of the spine, besides supporting the abdomen.

(3) The lateral muscles : These muscles lie at the sides of the trunk forming the lateral (side) wall of the abdomen. They run in a criss-cross manner and help control the sideward bending of the spine.

(4) The hip muscles : There are four groups of muscles performing as one unit for each hip. They are :

The hip flexors which are located at the front of the hip, attached to the front of the pelvis above and the front of the thigh-bone below. The most important of hip flexors is the psoas major muscle which not only moves the thigh forward but also acts as a giant sling to prevent the body from falling forward. When strains are imposed on this muscle, tremendous and irritating forces are exerted on the lumbar spine.

The hip adductors which are located at the outer sides of the hip.

The hip adductors which are located at the inner sides of the hip (groin).

The hip extensors which are massive muscles at the back of the hip, the most important being gluteus maximus which forms the buttocks.

These are the four sets of muscles that work together to support the spine. The pelvic foundation on which the lower spine rests is balanced by a controlled contraction of these muscles. If you recall that the spine is in proper working alignment when the pelvis is in the balanced position, you will be able to readily understand that these four interdependent groups of muscles must all be working properly. If any of these muscles is weak either because it is too short or too long, the spine will not be in proper alignment and there will be extra wear and tear on it increasing the probability of back pain.

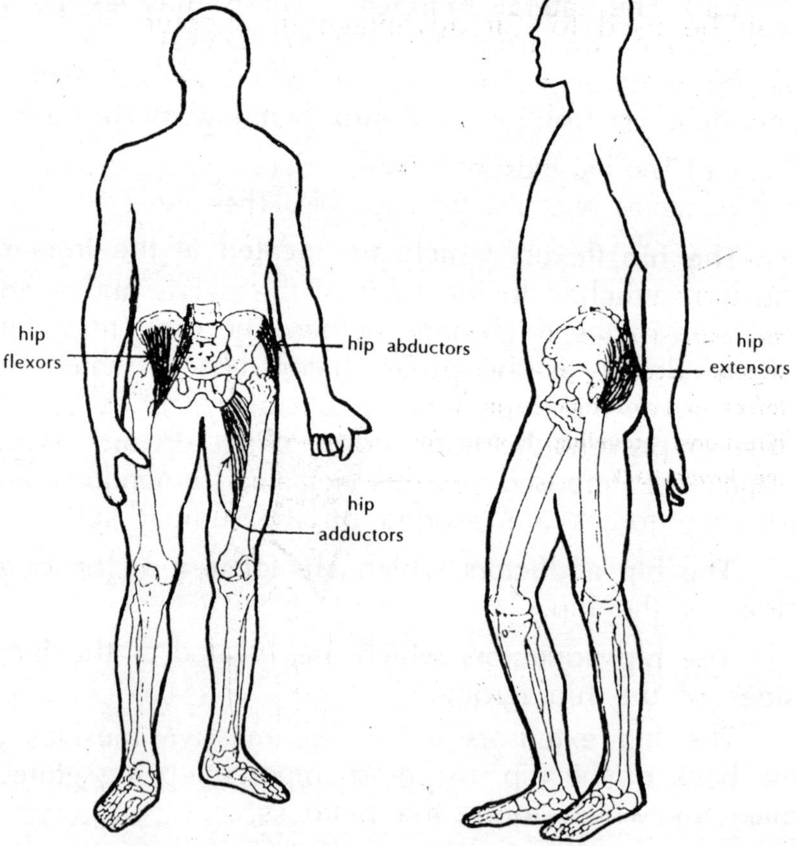

Fig. 2.9 : Muscles acting on the hip joint

Then there is a fascinating mechanism that provides extra support to the spine. It is called the hydraulic sac mechanism and is created by the co-ordinated contraction of stomach muscles, back muscles, the diaphragm and the pelvic floor muscles. When these muscles tighten simultaneously, the abdominal cavity, which is an enclosed sac of fluid, air and organs, gives added support to the spine. For example, when the spine is called on to lift a heavy load, the hydraulic sac helps equalise the effort so that the total weight of the load is not transmitted entirely through the spine but is distributed throughout the abdominal cavity. We will see how this hydraulic sac can be used to our advantage in chapter 9.

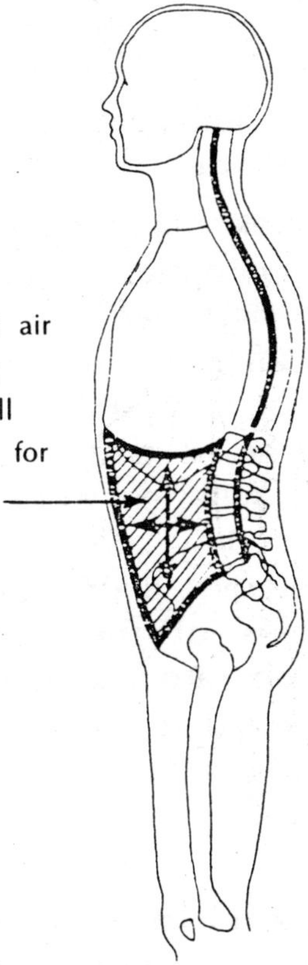

The hydraulic sac mechanism

Fig. 2.10

It has been stated earlier that a muscle is weakened if it becomes shorter or longer than its normal size.

A muscle lengthens if continuously stretched over a period, a common example being the stretching of abdominal muscles during pregnancy. When the abdominal muscles are thus weakened, other muscles that control the back are overburdened, resulting into discomfort, pain or even spasm.

A muscle shortens if it remains in a state of continuous contraction over a period. For example, following an injury to the back (or any other part of the body), the back muscles go into spasm, which is a protective reaction to prevent movement. A muscle in spasm is in a contracted state. Even after the injury has healed and pain has subsided, the muscles tend to remain shortened and weak.

We don't think many people realize that unless they undertake appropriate steps, especially exercises, to recondition lengthened (e.g., after pregnancy) or shortened (e.g., after an injury) muscles, their backs will be even more susceptible to problems than before. The reason for this is that before the pregnancy or the injury, back muscles were of optimum working lengths. But now they are shorter or longer, hence weaker and, therefore, liable to putting undue stress on other muscles of the back. Unless vigorous reconditioning steps are taken, the weakened back is susceptible to repeated or chronic trauma (injury). In a sedentary society, our muscles are not strong enough; even the slightest of unusual exertion may strain weak muscles.

Thus, for a backache patient, the only hope of total recovery lies in physical reconditioning. That is why a doctor can't prevent future backaches unless the patient is willing and determined to do his or her share of work. Fortunately, the 'Back Fitness Test' described in chapter 6 will quickly point out which of your back muscles need reconditioning. Thereafter, chapters 7, 8 and 9 will enlighten you on how to strengthen your back and then maintain it that way for the rest of your life. You will then be in a position to say, "Goodbye forever, backache !" and you would mean it.

---

3. THE CAUSES OF BACKACHE

There was a time when we were as confused as our patients about the real cause of low back pain. Misled by popular beliefs and prevalent concepts, we attributed every other backache to a degeneration (osteoarthritis) of the spine or a 'slipped' intervertebral disc. Well, we do not mean to say we now know everything about backs. The human back still remains something of an enigma. The reason for this that the back is one of the most complicated parts of the human body with dozens of ligaments, bones, muscles, nerves and blood vessels, fitted together in the most intricate way. Indeed, it would be extremely difficult, perhaps impossible, to design or construct a piece of machinery like that. Besides, the structures of the back are inaccessible to direct vision. Nowadays, a number of organs (viz. the stomach, the bladder, the rectum, the abdominal cavity, and even the insides of large joints) can be inspected or visualized using slim, telescope–like instruments. But there is no way by which a doctor can look into your back and tell you what, precisely, is going on there. It should be noted that X-rays are not of much help in diagnosing the cause of back problems as most people imagine. By and large, X-rays show only bones and are of little or no use in demonstrating what is going on in the soft tissues of the back such as muscles and ligaments which, as we shall see, are most of the times responsible for the pain. Thanks to such practical difficulties, it is said (albeit, in a lighter vein) in medical circles that, 'Doctors are better at managing a backache than determining its cause !' Therefore, if your doctor cannot diagnose or arrive at an opinion regarding the precise cause of your backache, don't think he or she is incompetent.

We can say that a lot more things, regarding the causes of backache, are clear today. But before discussing them, let us take a look at two interesting case histories.

* * *

27 years old Shankar Bhosle hailing from a small village near Pune in Maharashtra came to Bombay some five years ago in search of work. He came from a family of farmers. But his family had gradually grown bigger (with his elder brothers marrying) and now the small farm was no longer able to support all of them.

Virtually illiterate, Shankar was incapable of any white collar job. For one year, he did a variety of manual jobs including lifting heavy luggage at Bombay Central Railway Station. He ate no more than two meals a day mostly comprising of cooked dal (aamtee) and coarse bread or rice purchased from roadside stalls or small hotels. At night, he slept on footpaths which accommodate lakhs of less fortunate ones. During one year, he saved enough money to buy a hand-cart and rent a small hut in a hutment colony near Sion. Needless to say, life here was inhuman and unbearable, with open gutters breeding countless mosquitos, heaps of garbage everywhere and a tension-laden atmosphere created by antisocial elements. Diseases like malaria and dysentery were rampant in the whole colony.

To add to the already existing troubles, Shankar received demoralizing news that his father had an attack of paralysis. Thus, Shankar was now obliged to send some money regularly to his native place. He toiled day in and day out ignoring scorching sunshine or torrential rains while pulling his overloaded handcart. During the next four years, his weight reduced by ten kg. This was the natural result of relentless labour and unnourishing diet coupled with periodic attacks of malaria and almost perennial dysentery. Shankar did experience mild pain or stiffness in his knees at the end of an unduly hard day. But he never even once suffered from a backache. The same was the case with all other labourers with whom he had built friendship over the years.

* * *

The first time that Amit Desai, the only son of a self-made industrialist from Bombay, suffered from an attack of back pain was when he was lying on the golden sands of a beach in Tithal, a sea resort near Valsad in Gujarat. He had just appeared in the XII standard examination and was sent by his father to Valsad (where his uncle stayed) to enjoy a vacation. Amit just could not believe it had happened to him — it seemed ridiculous to have a backache at the age of 17. When he tried to get up, he doubled over with pain and had to be half carried to his uncle's residence. A doctor put him on pain-killers and tranquilizers. So here he was, lying flat on his back for three days, staring at the ceiling fan and wondering if this was the vacation he had dreamed of.

Who wouldn't opt to be the part of the best–fed, best–schooled, best–dressed crowd if one had a chance? But the life of a rich man's son is not always as wonderful as it looks to an outsider. Amit's life, definitely, was not a bed of roses. He just could not live upto his stern father's expectations.

Amit passed the XII examination with flying colours. He had a great liking for mathematics but had to take up law because it was his father's opinion that a sound knowledge of law would help them in their business. It was a tough course but Amit did not mind the long hours of study. He engaged himself in sports, especially badminton, on Sundays and believed he was in good shape. Indeed, he had no memories of the first attack of back pain. He enjoyed the next two and a half years studying and playing. He was mystified when he had a second bout of backache while driving non-stop to Khandala, a small hill-station near Bombay. However, like the first attack, it was relieved after a few days of rest and was soon forgotten.

Amit passed the final LL.B. examination at the age of 21 and immediately joined his father in business. Life, thereafter, was fairly pleasant for him except for the fact that he could not help disliking the ways of his father, who was a tall, aggressive and dominating man. Amit felt disgusted at the way his father dictated to his employees. He had made up his mind never to handle people that way. He was slowly developing a personality opposite to that of his father. He did not even want to resemble his father physically.

At the age of 26, Amit was married to Smita, a happy-go-lucky girl of his age. A psychology graduate, she was the first person to opine that he had an inferiority complex which was manifesting in his rounded shoulders and a slouching posture. A careful observation in the mirror made him realize that Smita was not kidding.

In his early thirties, Amit started experiencing stiffness in his back in mornings or after long car-drives. A hard day in a tennis court or a golf course brought on a lot of back twinges and discomfort. He attributed these developments to the rising business stress and the increasing work-load.

It happened again when Amit had just turned 34. He was playing badminton on a Sunday morning when his back gave way. It was sheer agony. He had to be carried home. The diagnosis was low back pain due to sudden ligamental injury. His back muscles had gone into a spasm (an involuntary and continuous contracted state) to splint the injured area of his back. He felt nervous and scared. It took long time before he could move again without pain. But this attack left him thinking. Should he decrease his work-load ? Should he continue with sports or give up ? Should he continue to engage in vigorous sex with his wife ? Was he to suffer from such attacks again and again ? Was there any way of preventing further attacks ?

* * *

Here we have two young men of approximately the same age. One is living in terrible conditions, suffering from malnutrition and required to work like a beast, pulling loads unheard of in normal circumstances. Yet he never once suffered from a backache. The other young man is living under enviable conditions – in fact, he was on a vacation when his first back pain came – and yet he has a recurrent back problem that seems bent to alter his life. Is this man's backache really caused by stress as he firmly believes ?

If so, why did he get his first attack while he was relaxing on a seashore ? It seems he has discounted the episodes that occurred earlier. He should not. They were the first warnings that he was in for more trouble later on. Attacks of low back pain are indication to the fact that the back is not in a good condition and needs strengthening. Let us again return to the factor of stress. There is no doubt that Amit's work does have stressful elements; but surely, Shankar was living in more stressful conditions. He spent every day in a struggle for physical survival–his own and that of his family at his native place. Why did he not get a backache ? Could Amit's back pain be the outcome of a heavy work load ? The question seems redundant if we consider the hard work put in by Shankar. Does Amit have back trouble because his bed is too soft or his car-seat not properly adjusted ? Remember that Shankar slept on footpaths and could not afford even bus-rides. Could it be age, could it be heredity or could it just be plain bad luck ? Or could the cause be something so simple as to escape the minds of most sufferers, even doctors ? Could Amit's backache, and yours, be the result of poor posture and week muscles ?

We are sure some of these questions must have sprung up in your mind, too. These are the same questions that started haunting our minds and led us to our new, preventive approach to back-care, which we have, since, put into practice to obtain gratifying results.

The possibility that weak muscles and poor posture (which are the outcome of sedentary habits of civilised (?) humans), when subjected to physical and mental strains of modern life, react by going into spasm and produce pain dawned upon us a few years back while successively examining two backache patients.

The first was a pregnant woman. The second was an obese male patient with a pot belly. He had suffered from back pain for the third time in a few months. While examining him, we realized that he looked as pregnant as the lady who had just left our clinic. The lady was eventually going to lose the weight on her abdomen and would return to normal provided she took exercises for her stretched muscles. The man, however, was not going to lose his pot belly unless he took some drastic action. On examination, it was evident that this man's lower back had a steep hollow, his abdominal muscles were lax and his back muscles were in spasm. Thereafter, we started examining the back muscles of all our patients, whether they had a backache or not. We noticed a definite inter-relation between spasm of back muscles and back pain. In other words, muscle spasm is the cause of low back pain in most (almost ninety per cent) patients. Further still, spastic muscles may pull the spine in an abnormal shape, resulting into mechanical disadvantage and chances of more trouble.

Patients are bewildered when they first hear the word 'spasm'. Let us take the case of Mr. Kulkarni who recently consulted us.

"What is muscle spasm, doctor ?", he asked.

"Mr. Kulkarni, have you ever suffered from cramps in your leg, especially at night ?", we posed a counter question.

"Yes, they are very painful and the muscles remain sore for a number of days thereafter," he replied.

"Well, that is muscle spasm. Now just try to imagine the muscles of your back contracted in the same way. Because of this continuous contracted state, the small blood vessels that supply nutrients to the muscles or that drain away waste products are squeezed shut. It is because of such accumulation of waste products and cutting off of nutrition that muscles in the spasm become very tender and painful," we said.

"Mr. Kulkarni, make the strongest fist you can and keep holding it."

After some seconds he said, "It is beginning to get tired."

"Keep holding it," we said.

"It is becoming uncomfortable," he said after some time.

"Keep holding it," we reiterated.

"It has started paining," he finally said.

"Okay, release it. We just wanted you to realize how any muscle which remains contracted for a long time, first tires and then hurts."

"But why, in the first place does a muscle go into spasm ?" he inquired.

We explained to him that muscle spasm, in a sense, is a protective mechanism. It can be triggered by a number of factors like obesity, a sudden jerk or strain from lifting, stretching or an accident resulting into an injury to ligaments, joints or bones in the spine, prolonged immobility, incorrect body-position while driving or reading, pregnancy or even a psychological cause like nervous tension, depression, anxiety, fear, etc. (More about this in chapter 9.) But one thing is certain : these precipitating factors are rendered ineffective if the various muscles associated with the back are strong so that they always hold the pelvis in a balanced position.

"But why do these muscles weaken ?" Mr. Kulkarni's inquisitive mind was still not at rest.

"Backache can be termed as a hypokinetic disease," we said, "which means that inactivity and a sedentary life-style are major factors contributing to it. It is a well-known fact that muscles, if not sufficiently used, turn flabby and weak."

"Then why do some persons of our company, having jobs involving physical labour, suffer from backaches ?" he retorted, and his question was quite logical.

"Well, hard physical labour would give the back muscles the workout they need to keep the back in shape only if a job called for fairly constant exertion. However, most of the industries and factories require labourers to do only intermittent or sporadic heavy work. A truck driver, for example, who sits for most of the day and then unloads his vehicle at the end of a long trip is a prime candidate for muscle-injury and spasm and, therefore, backache."

The look of Mr. Kulkarni's face clearly indicated that he was still not fully convinced about the fact that as simple a thing as muscle spasm was at the root of most backaches. He is not alone in such attitude. It is not surprising. After all, it has been hammered into people's minds that backaches are due to disc problems and arthritis of the spine (spondylosis !). The fact remains, however, that disc problems, osteoarthritis and all other defects and diseases put together cannot account for more than ten per cent of all backaches !

Let us, then, have a brief and simplified overview of the various conditions that go to make up the paltry ten per cent causes of backache.

(1) Osteoarthritis of the spine (lumbar spondylosis) : In spite of the ominous-sounding words, this means no more than degeneration or wear and tear process of the spine because of ageing.

Winston Churchill described ageing as 'the stealthy advance of surly decrepitude'. But an alternative and kinder definition would be : Ageing is a slow, gentle advance in maturity, wisdom and experience, accompanied by an increasing inelasticity of soft tissues, wearing of cartilages and a variable thinning of the texture of the bones of the body. Well, the spine is no exception; it is liable to the same degenerative changes that occur in the rest of the body.

Degeneration of the spine is characterized by : (a) a narrowing of the invertebral joint space (due to the thinning of the disc), (b) formation of osteophytes (new bony spurs) at the margins of vertebral bodies and (c) the swelling of the posterior facet joints.

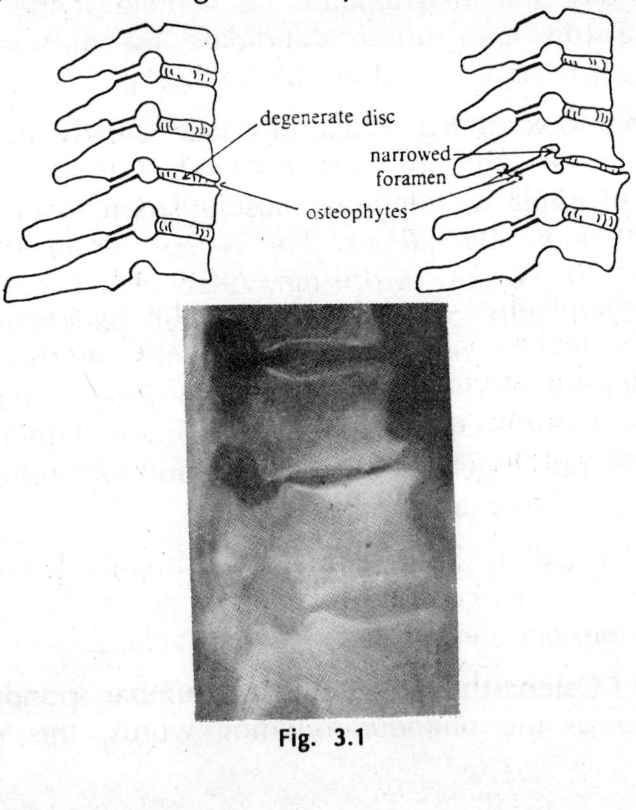

Fig. 3.1

Degeneration starts in everybody of us by the age of 25 or 30. By the age of 60, it is quite advanced so that few of us have normal spinal X-rays, a fact to be understood and kept in mind.

As a general rule, osteoarthritis of the spine is not serious and usually asymptomatic.

In a few persons, however, it may give rise to slight stiffness, mild intermittent pain or sometimes, grating. But it is far too insignificant a cause of back trouble than people believe.

(2) 'Slipped' disc : Although there is, in reality, no such thing as a 'slipped' disc, the term has become a part of modern usage. There is no way a disc can actually slip out of place. It merely bulges when there is too much pressure or a sudden shearing strain on the spine. Therefore, many doctors prefer to use other synonyms of this word, like herniated disc, prolapsed disc, ruptured disc, bulging disc, sequestrated disc, protruding disc and extruded disc.

That a disc could herniate and protrude was not realized till 1934 AD. Two Harvard professors : Mixter, a neurosurgeon and Barr, an orthopedic surgeon were the first to present a report on disc herniation, documenting the condition clinically as well as microscopically. They claimed that the nucleus pulposus can squeeze out of its normal site and press on surrounding structures, for example, roots of the sciatic nerve, causing pain.

Herniation of the disc is, usually (though by no means always), the result of some sudden violent episode such as a fall, an accident, strain while lifting a heavy object, a twisting jerk of the trunk, etc.

A herniated disc occurs in about five to seven per cent of backaches and is diagnosed by a doctor when the following conditions exist :

The patient complains of pain radiating or shooting down into the leg (along the course of the sciatic nerve which is being irriated by the impingement or pressure) and muscle weakness. During an examination, the patient may be unable to raise the leg without pain (thus, a positive 'straight leg raising' test). Then, there may be changes of sensations in the leg, such as numbness, tingling (pins and needles) or alterations in knee and ankle reflexes. In more serious cases, there may be loss of tone in sphincter muscles of the bladder and the bowel, and loss of sensation in the rectal area. This is a medical emergency requiring immediate treatment. Fortunately, it is extremely rare.

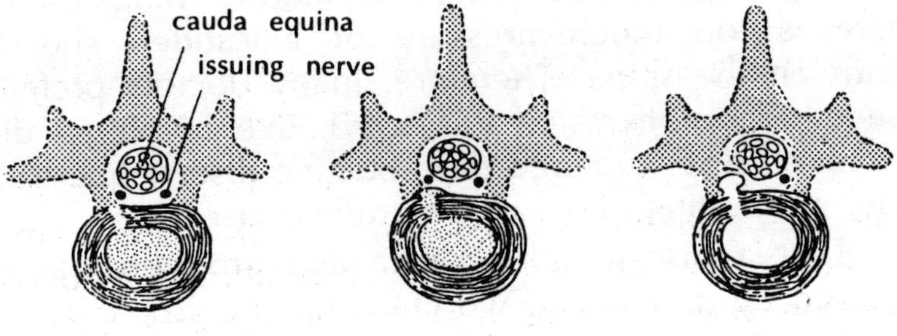

Fig. 3.2

A conclusive diagnosis of a herniated disc is not possible from a plain X-ray picture. Unless a myelogram, a venogram or other sophisticated tests are done, no doctor can make a diagnosis of a so-called 'slipped' disc. These tests sometimes become necessary when a patient's pain cannot be relieved by conservative treatment over a period of weeks or when there is an increasing loss of nerve function in the affected leg.

A herniated disc is usually a progressive condition. It would be no exaggeration to say that in most cases, it is not the beginning of back trouble but the end-result of a process, the warning signs of which have been conveniently ignored. It is simply the final thing that happens to a system that has been out of balance for a number of years.

(3) Sudden strain or injury caused by lifting something the wrong way : It is human nature to want to attribute a problem to something concrete, something we can come to grips with and avoid in future. That is the reason why almost all back sufferers are querried by their doctors regarding some unaccustomed labour or lifting of some heavy weight awkwardly. Now there is no doubt that lifting objects the right way will minimize the risks of back pain (in fact, we have devoted chapter 9 to proper lifting and working techniques). But what we wish to emphasize here is that a lifting episode, in most cases, was simply the straw that broke the camel's back. The real problem was present since long.

Let us consider a study to illustrate our point. The predominant type of low back injury among workers of a very big factory was attributed to over-exertion which means that the employee's back was too weak to handle a task or, conversely, that the task was too great even for the employee with a strong back. However, the study revealed that 62 per cent of low back injuries fell into that category while the rest 38 per cent were caused by falling objects, slips or falls, and unknown causes. Further questioning showed that only 26 per cent of the employees in the over-exertion classification had injured their backs while lifting objects. The other's could not give a definite cause for their backache. Backaches are not usually caused, as we would like to think, by lifting something the wrong way. In most cases, backaches are caused by weak muscles that rebel against the overwork and strain by going into sustained contraction or spasm.

(4) Structural defect of the spine : Surprisingly large number of people, about half the population according to one widely accepted estimate, have minor congenital defects of the spine and its associated structures. Therefore, it would be an exaggeration to call them defects. They can be better termed 'physiological variations'. They include scoliosis, kyphosis, lordosis, spondylolisthesis and spina bifida. Only occasionally do these conditions cause discomfort or backache.

Scoliosis is an abnormal lateral deviation of the spine so that when viewed from behind, the victim's spine shows a sideward bend.

Kyphosis, commonly termed 'a round back' or 'a hump back' is a condition in which the backward curvature of the thoracic spine is excessive.

Lordosis is a condition in which the forward curvature of the lumbar spine is excessive. In other words, there is an exaggerated sway or hollow of the spine.

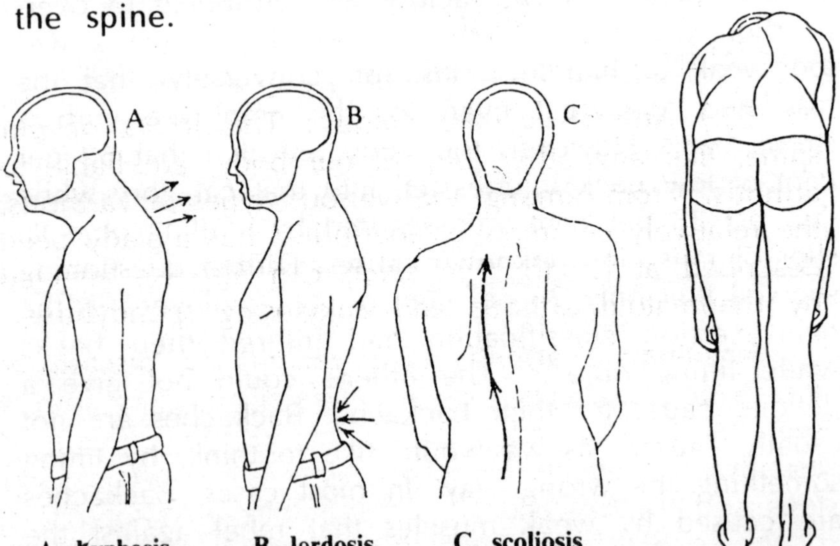

A. Kyphosis B. lordosis C. scoliosis rib hump

Fig. 3.3

Spondylolisthesis is a rare condition in which there is a displacement (usually forward) of one vertebra with respect to the next lower vertebra. It is thus a 'slipping' of a vertebra over the next lower vertebra. The word is a tongue twister. You may even dare your doctor to pronounce it fast; he is likely to fumble !

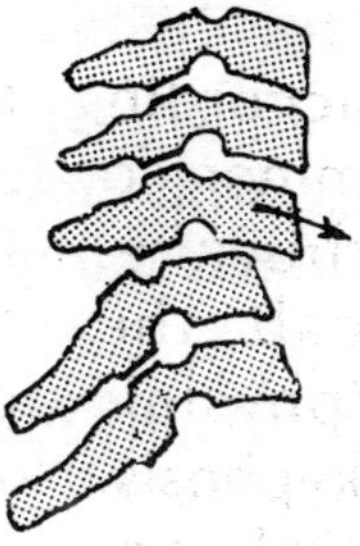

Fig 3.4

Spina bifida is again a rare condition in which there is a structural defect in the back part of one or more of the vertebrae, is shown in the figures below. Thus the spinal cord remains slightly or severely unprotected.

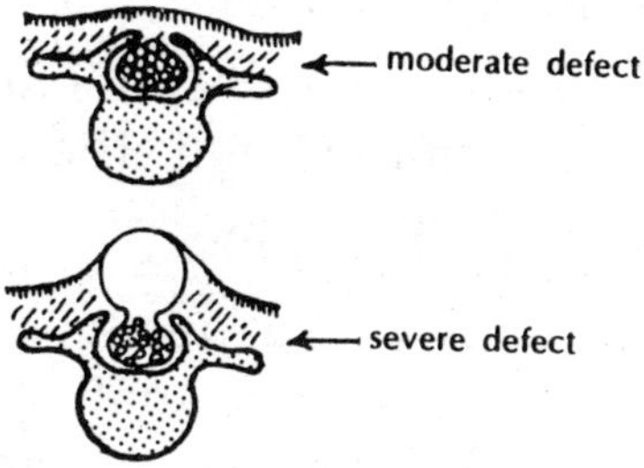

Fig. 3.5

(5) Arthritis of the spine : The joints of our spine, like any other joint of our body, are liable to arthritis. From among the various types of arthritis, the relatively common 'osteoarthritis' has already been described at length. The spine can also be affected by rheumatoid arthritis and ankylosing spondylitis.

Rheumatoid arthritis is a generalized disease of the body. It affects women more than men and is seen most often in persons aged 20 to 35 years. It usually first affects the small joints of the fingers and toes and then spreads to other joints including those of the spine. The cause of this disease is still a matter of conjecture.

Ankylosing spondylitis is an ill-understood disease of the spine which affects men (between ages of 20 to 30 years) more often than women and causes pain in, and severe stiffness of, the whole spine. The spinal ligaments are ossified (transformed into bones) so that the spine virtually becomes a rigid tube. A victim of ankylosing spondylitis acquires a stooping posture, commonly called a 'poker back'.

(6) Metabolic diseases like osteoporosis (a generalized thinning or rarefaction of bones) or gout (a disease of deranged purine metabolism) may occasionally cause a backache.

(7) Localized diseases of the spine, e.g., Paget's disease, osteomyelitis.

(8) Infections of the spine, including tuberculous arthritis, pyogenic arthritis and rheumatoid arthritis.

(9) Tumours of the spine

(10) Visceral causes like peptic ulcer, pancreatitis, kidney infections, kidney stone, gall stone, cholecystitis (swelling of the gall bladder), cervicitis (swelling of the neck of the uterus), salpingitis (swelling of fallopian tubes) etc. may produce backaches.

(11) Vascular (blood-circulatory) causes like Leriche's syndrome (a clot in the abdominal aorta) or aneurysm of the abdominal aorta may give rise to pain which mimics a backache.

(12) Psychological causes : The sub-heading might come to you as a surprise. The fact remains, however, that psychological problems can sometimes cause and often aggravate backaches.

You may not realize how intimately your body and mind are inter-related. Separating bodily aches from the more ethereal aches of the soul is a less straightforward task than you might think.

It is not rare for severely depressed or anxiety-affected patients to focus on the lower back as the source of their pain. These patients are neither 'faking' nor 'carping', because to them, the pain 'feels' absolutely real.

In one American survey of depressed patients attending the psychiatric clinic of a big hospital, around half the patients had initially some 'rheumatic' complaint which, in fact, was a part of, and due to, their depression, and the majority of these complaints were of backache.

Given below are some other examples of subtle psychological causes producing backaches :

The 'you owe me' back pain : Insurance companies who have to deal with accident-compensation cases sometimes come across this phenomenon. The backache lasts until all legal and financial questions of a compensation case are settled, and then miraculously disappears.

Please note again that the patient does actually feel the pain.

The 'I need treatment' back pain : When a patient consults a doctor about back pain, the real problem could lie elsewhere. The patient might have a sexual problem but is too embarrassed to talk about it. Alternatively, he or she might suspect the presence of some serious disease, may want it diagnosed but may be afraid to mention it. In effect, the patient is telling the doctor, 'I am ill; but I want you to discover the real problem by yourself'.

The 'excuse me' back pain : A backache can be made to serve as an explanation or excuse for some failure.

The 'all-purpose cop out' : Backaches may be used to remain away from unpleasant tasks or unwelcome social obligations.

"I am afraid you will have to run the meeting without me; my back seems to be acting up again."

"I was planning to take you out to a movie and dinner, but my back...."

"You know how much I wanted to do it tonight, but my back pain....."

The 'I have emotional problem' backache : Any type of emotional problem may give rise to physical complaints like backache, headache, etc. Indeed, many diseases are nowadays considered psychosomatic (psyche = mind; soma = body).

* * *

It is quite probable that longstanding psychological problems and chronic mental stress bring about a chronic tension in the body-muscles. And back, rendered vulnerable due to our sedentary life-style, becomes the victim of pain.

It should be noted that all backaches, irrespective of their causes, give rise to a certain amount of anxiety and mental tension which, in turn, aggravate the back pain. Thus, a vicious circle is formed.

* * *

Well, that brings us to an end of the discussion about the less common causes of back pain. This list of causes, though by no means complete, is fairly exhaustive. All of these causes put together do not account for more than ten per cent of all backaches. The important and real cause of most backaches is poor posture combined with weak muscles resulting into a spasm of back muscles.

This chapter should not be used for self-diagnosis of the cause of a back problem. As we have shown, some backaches are because of some disease or some mechanical derangement of the spine, which may require precise diagnosis and urgent treatment. Otherwise the problem can worsen.

---

4. EXAMINATION AND INVESTIGATIONS FOR DIAGNOSIS

As is clear from the previous chapter, 90 per cent of all backaches are due to musculo-skeletal disorders or in layman's language, muscle spasm. Only in the rest 10 per cent patients is the backache due to some disease or structural defect of the spine, or a systemic cause.

While we can't urge you strongly enough to seek proper diagnosis and treatment of any pain that stays with you for more than 3–4 weeks or which progressively gets worse, take comfort in the knowledge that even persistent backaches seldom spell dire malady. Hence, don't lose any sleep worrying about serious or mysterious diseases.

The diagnosis of the cause of backache is one of exclusion–more aimed at ascertaining the absence of certain conditions or diseases than at ascertaining the presence of one. It still remains largely a matter of clinical (i.e., physical) examination.

Before actual physical examination, any doctor will like to have answers to the following questions :

(1) Have you had back trouble before ?

(2) Since how long is the present pain troubling you ?

(3) Did it come suddenly or did it build up gradually ?

(4) What were you doing when the present pain started ?

(5) Had you put your back under any kind of unaccustomed stress in the few days before the pain came on ?

(6) Is your job or a hobby such as would place abnormal strain on your back ?

(7) In which part of the back, precisely, did the pain start ? Where is it located now ? Has it spread ?

(8) Is there any pain in the front or the back of the thigh ?

(9) Does the pain radiate (spread) below the knee and into the foot ?

(10) What activities relieve or aggravate this pain ?

(11) Have other symptoms like fever, joint pains and muscle pains accompanied the back pain ?

The answers to these questions offer clues that help to determine whether a patient is suffering from referred pain or whether the pain is due to nerve-root irritation in the spine.

Since back pain is a symptom and not a disease, the source of the pain may lie outside the spine. Although this occurs in only a small percentage of cases, it is for that reason a doctor asks back-patients for the family history of certain diseases as well as other questions relating to changes in bowel habits or in the appetite, abnormal bleeding, weight-loss and chronic cough.

The next step of examination entails observation of the overall posture : whether the spine is straight or tilted to one side (scoliosis), whether one side of the body is favoured more than the other and whether there is a sag in one of the buttocks. The stride is also observed to detect abnormality, if any. Movements of the spine are observed to note any limitation of range due to pain.

Next, the patient is taken to the examination table. This actual examination entails :

(1) Determination of knee and ankle reflexes by tapping specific tendons with a reflex hammer,

(2) Assessing muscle power by performing certain movements,

(3) Ascertaining the intactness of nerve–function by checking the sensations in the lower leg with pin-pricks,

(4) Passively raising the legs (one at a time) of the patient to detect a possible disc disorder,

(5) Asking the patient to draw his / her knees to the chest to know if there is tightness or spasm of low back muscles,

(6) Checking the buttocks for muscle tone and sensation,

(7) Palpating the back and the spine for muscle spasm, lumps, tenderness or an abnormal curve,

(8) Examining the rectum to check for growths, swellings and the position of the cervix and to evaluate the condition of the coccyx; in men, the prostate gland is also palpated during rectal examination,

(9) Examining the abdomen to detect an enlargement, if any, of the various organs.

That brings an end to the physical examination for determining the cause of backache.

Besides, in order to rule out the possibility of the small percentage of serious diseases like congenital scoliosis, spina bifida, osteoporosis, ankylosing spondylitis, rheumatoid arthritis, abscess, tuberculosis or cancerous tumours of the spine, gynacological conditions or prostatitis, the doctor may advise investigation of the urine and the blood or may recommend an X–ray of the spine.

However, patients tend to over-emphasize the importance of X–rays. And doctors are to be blamed for such a state of affairs. We can assure you that once a serious disease has been ruled out, an X–ray tells the doctor very little. By and large, X–rays show only bones, and are of little or no use in demonstrating what is going on in the soft tissues of the back such as muscles, ligaments and tendons. This is an unfortunate aspect of X–rays in that they cause people to overemphasize the importance of bones in the spine, while neglecting to consider the equally (perhaps more) critical part played by the muscles of the back.

Dr. Ian McNab, a world authority on modern back surgery explains in his book, 'Backache', that because of the difficulties in diagnosing the cause of low back pain, there was a period when physicians laid the blame for inexplicable symptoms on the diverse and curious anomalies of the spine revealed on an X–ray. When it was later discovered that these anatomical variations occurred just as frequently in the population at large as in those with backache, it was evident that they could not be considered the sole cause of backache.

How often have you heard someone say, "My X–ray showed a spinal defect that is causing my backache," or "My backache is caused by a degenerating disc which showed up on an X–ray." Yet Dr. McNab has pointed out that a study of the X–rays of 300 labourers showed no difference in the incidence of degenerative changes in the spines although 150 complained of backache and were under treatment whereas the other 150 had never had a backache. The fact is that degenerative disc disease, a normal part of the aging process, begins in all of us after the age of 25 years. Again, most people in the course of their lives injure their spine at some time or another by falling down or by lifting heavy weights and the discs in these affected areas may show evidence of old injury in X–rays taken later. More commonly, simple twists or strains produce similar injuries to the cartilagenous discs between vertebrae so that, by the age of 60 years, few of us have normal X–rays.

To conclude, we would advise you to beware of needless X-rays. A routine set of spine X-rays in a young woman, for example, has a radiation effect on her ovaries equivalent to chest X–rays administered daily for sixty days !

---

5. THE TREATMENT OF BACKACHE

The only thing that backache patients crave for, is quick and lasting relief from pain. When in acute pain, a sermon about posture and habits sounds like foul talk to their ears. Well, that is not surprising at all. Pain is one of the worst of human afflictions, robbing people of the will to work, to create and to accomplish anything in life. Indeed, back pain is a malevolent dictator that robs its victim of the full enjoyment of life. For persons with a chronic backache, pain is such a frustrating and debilitating problem that it becomes almost a disease in itself.

Thus, the first aim of the treatment of any back problem is to alleviate pain. Pain stimulates muscle spasm; muscle spasm, in turn, intensifies pain. Thus, a vicious circle is formed that tends to worsen matters. The earlier this cycle is interrupted, the better for the patient as well as his back, which will heal faster.

There are three types or degrees of back pain, each with different characters. The first is 'acute' pain which is sharp, intense, sudden and unexpected, the kind you feel if you suffer the misfortune of hitting your thumb with a hammer. The second type is 'chronic' pain which is long-standing, usually dull and unremitting. The third type, 'mild pain', is not pain in true sense but just discomfort and stiffness. We will have little to say of such back discomfort except that it may be a gentle reminder to the sufferer that all is not well with the back and preventive action must be contemplated without delay.

We shall consider the treatment of backache under two subheadings : 'Treatment of acute back pain' and 'Treatment of chronic back pain'.

Treatment of acute back pain : Because of no apparent reason (as is many a time the case) or because of something you did (for example, while playing tennis, you hit a forceful cross-court shot or you lifted a tyre out of the dickey of your car and twisted around to put it on the ground or perhaps you simply bent over from your chair to pick up a paper clip) which resulted into sudden wrenching, jarring or jolting of the spine, you have been hit by acute low back pain. What, now, should be done ?

What is the best course of action in the first few hours after an attack ? These are important questions.

Pain is usually equated with harmful disease. An episode of acute pain creates panic in the mind of most persons. They run helter-skelter for medical help. They summon their family physician even if it is the middle of the night, insisting that he or she should come at once. Alternatively, they put in frantic efforts to obtain an urgent appointment with an orthopaedic surgeon. At the other extreme, there are heroes (or heroines) who disregard the warning signal and manfully (!) plod on, thinking that the sun will be stuck below the horizon if they don't continue to work. In doing so, they wreck their backs.

"Well, what is the correct course of action ? Should a person in acute pain not consult a doctor ?" You are sure to ask.

In reply, we will say that as long as you do not have trouble in passing urine or you don't feel distinct weakness in your legs, you can manage the attack YOURSELF ! On the other hand, if there is evidence that you are fast losing control over your urinary bladder or that your leg muscles are getting increasingly weaker, it is a medical emergency, which may even require urgent surgery. But such incidents are extremely rare, indeed.

(1) Bed-rest : The most important immediate step (you may call it 'first aid' if you wish) following an attack of acute back pain is to take complete bed-rest. "Just go to bed, doctor ? That is no treatment !" many patients exclaim. They are surprised (rather shocked) to discover that total rest is very good 'treatment' and all that is necessary in many, if not most, cases. Most backaches are due to muscle spasm resulting out of strains, sprains or tears, which, like a sprained ankle, need a period of rest followed by a period of rehabilitation and gradual mobilization. Bed-rest is truly treatment and not an idle or helpless 'giving—way' to things.

Therefore, if you get severe back pain, stop all physical activity right away. If the attack has hit you while you were playing on the ground or working in your office, head straight for your home immediately, preferably taking a car or a taxi rather than fighting your way there by public transport. If your employer is sensible, he probably won't mind—after all, it is better for both of you if you take about a week off at the right time rather than prolonged and indefinite offs and ons later on, as the problem becomes chronic.

Bed-rest literally means 'resting by lying in the bed'. It does not mean sitting around the house watching T.V.— that would be silly, indeed. But deciding to take bed-rest is not enough. Knowing how to lie down correctly, so that the injured muscles or ligaments get true rest, is vitally important. We have said earlier that the 'balanced pelvis' position is the position of health and strength for the back. It is also the position that is conducive to quick pain-relief and healing.

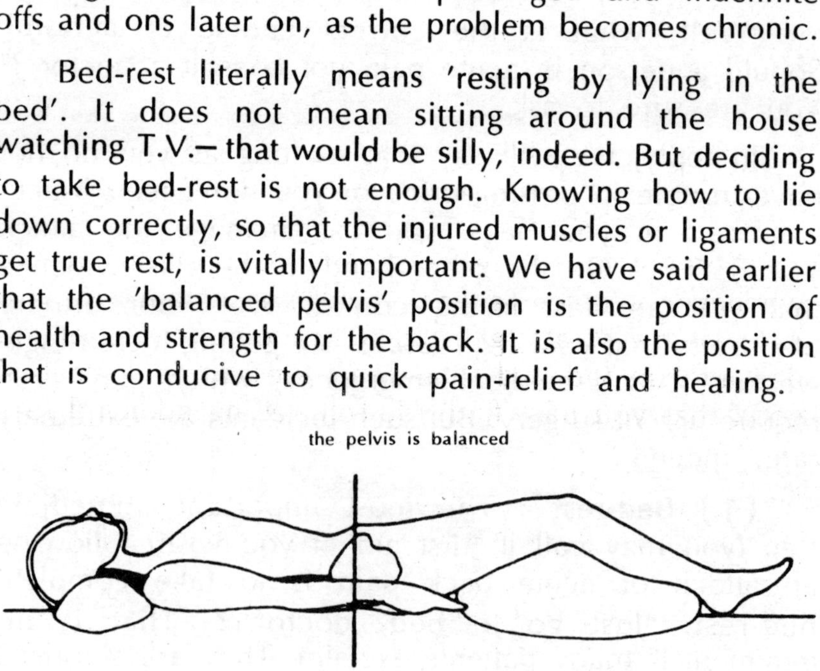

Good bed-rest positions

Fig. 5.1

The pelvis can be easily balanced in the bed. You should lie on the back with the head resting on a thin pillow and the lower legs kept elevated with the help of two or three pillows so that the hollow of the lower back is flattened out. The mattress should be firm so that the body is not allowed to sag. Many patients find that the floor is even more comfortable than the bed. The patient lies on the floor, with the legs elevated by keeping them on the edge of a sofa or a chair.

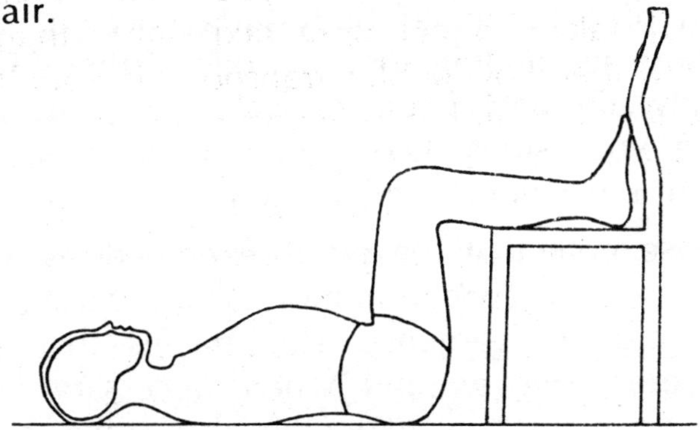

Fig. 5.2

This is also a good defensive position to take whenever you feel a back twinge is coming on. You can watch T.V. at night in this position after a strenuous day and unload and relax your tired spine. It feels so good that you may find yourself getting addicted to it.

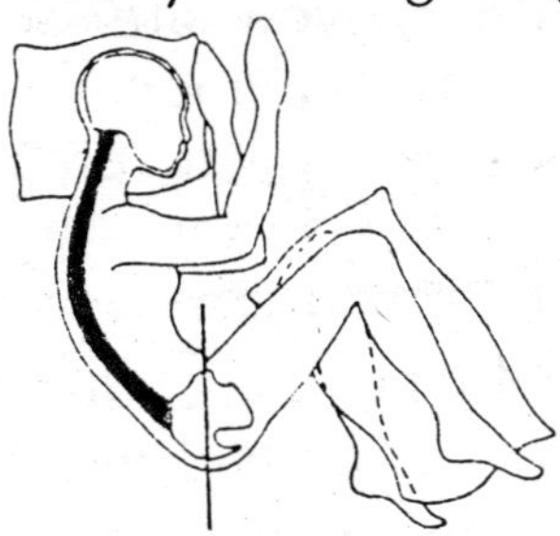

the foetal position : pillow between the knees to prevent twisting of the spine

Fig. 5.3

A sore back can also be rested and soothed by lying on your side. Roll over to one of your sides. Place your head on a pillow. Keep the knees and hips bent as much towards the chest as comfortable. Keep a pillow between the two knees to prevent the spine from being twisted.

In fact, no person can lie or sleep in one position for too long. Such changes of body-position prevent blood-stagnation and joint-stiffness and ensure that the skin of a particular body-surface is not subjected to pressure for unduly long periods of time. Therefore, frequently alternate between lying on your back and lying on your sides, taking care to keep your pelvis balanced (i.e., your lumbar hollow flattened).

Please note that the purpose of bed-rest is to rest the spine and prevent irritation of the spastic muscles or the injured ligaments. This means that you can move your arms as and when necessary. You can also move your feet (keeping the spine stationary) periodically, to ensure good circulation of blood in the vessels of the legs. Though it is desirable to pass water and open the bowels (using special containers) on the bed itself, you can carefully get up to go to the bathroom or lavatory if you wish so. But certainly do not get up to open the door, answer the telephone or prepare meals. If you are a housewife and all alone during the day, summon your sister or sister-in-law or hire a maid-servant to prepare meals and look after your house. Surely your house won't cease to be a house even if you don't work.

This last statement is intended to emphasize, once again the importance of bed-rest for back patients. If you don't take this advice, you stand the risk of further injuring your back or delaying your recovery. We are aware that busy people can't rest and relax easily. Some doctors have said that unless patients are confined in a plaster of Paris cast from head to heels (with a few holes, of course), they are unlikely to rest. Bed-rest can be supervised or forced in a hospital; but at home, you have to be your own disciplinarian.

Getting in and out of bed becomes an art when you are struck with a backache.

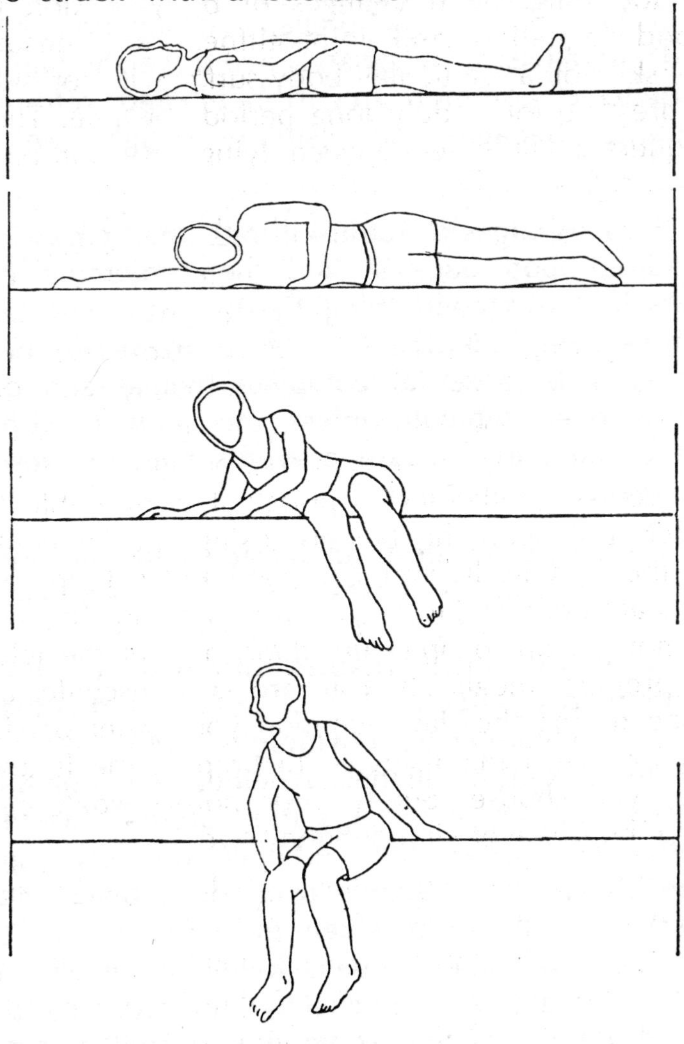

Fig. 5.4

To get out of the bed, first lie on your side, facing that side of the bed from which you plan to get down. Now, without twisting or bending your back, push up to the sitting position using your arms. At the same time, slide your legs over the edge of the bed to the floor. To get back into the bed reverse the sequence of movements.

While on bed-rest, prevent constipation (by using mild purgatives if necessary), avoid weight-gain (which is quite a common occurrence) and refrain from smoking (because the resultant cough can irritate the back).

(2) Analgesic (pain-killing) medicines : After deciding upon bed-rest and then enforcing it upon yourself, the second thing to do is to start taking a pain-relieving medicine. Such a medicine becomes necessary because (a) complete mental and physical rest is often difficult unless the pain is controlled and eased and (b) pain prevents an early resolution of muscle spasm.

Perhaps, the best analgesic medicine for back pain is aspirin. In cases associated with injury or disease (where there is inflammation), it can often produce dramatic results because of its anti-inflammatory effect. It is available individually as well as in combination with other pure analgesic or muscle-relaxant medicines. Whether such 'combination' drugs enjoy any advantage over ordinary aspirin is a controversial issue. But certainly, ordinary aspirin is quite cheap and available over the counter without a prescription. Aspiring, taken in doses of two tablets, three to four times a day, following meals or light snacks, usually proves effective in reducing pain. It should be noted that some manufacturers, who feel shy of disclosing that their tablets contain aspirin, use the synonym 'acetylsalicylic acid'.

Though cheap and effective, aspirin may produce side-effects, as every other drug on the earth can. It can produce stomach irritation, hyperacidity, gastritis or even ulcers in sensitive persons, especially if taken on an empty stomach. More seriously, it can cause bleeding inside the body.

The alternative to aspirin, then, is paracetamol, which when taken in doses of two tablets, three to four times a day, produces similar analgesic effects.

However, even paracetamol can produce undesirable side-effects, especially when taken in large doses.

These two things, i.e., bed-rest and pain-relieving medicines are the main-stays in the treatment of acute back pain.

At this point, the question of whether (or when) you should summon your doctor or not is likely to arise in your mind again. The question is quite difficult to answer; but, in general, there is nothing urgent or immediate that a doctor can do in the first few hours after an attack. But certainly, you should seek the advice of your doctor (by giving him a ring) if your pain does not reduce even after twelve hours, or has actually worsened.

Persons who can't stand or tolerate any medicine or who are apprehensive of their harmful side-effects, can successfully alleviate pain by stimulating (with finger-pressure) certain specific Acupressure points on their bodies. Even those persons who can tolerate medicines quite well can utilize these points to reinforce the effectivity of medicines or to cut down upon their dosage. Details about this Oriental mode of treatment, which is being extensively used in Western countries to relieve pain, have been given later in this chapter, while discussing the treatment of chronic back pain.

(3) Other home remedies : Heat has been used as a remedy for pain by every race throughout the history of mankind. Even animals seem to know that heat will relieve pain – watch an old rheumatic dog and see how it searches out the sunniest part of the yard to warm its bones. Heat improves the blood supply of the exposed part, so that the toxic wastes, accumulated in spastic muscles, are flushed away.

Anything that is handy can be used to deliver heat to your back : a hot water bag, a glass bottle, a heating pad or towels soaked in hot water. Expensive gadgets or appliances are not more useful in relieving pain.

Heat can be applied several times a day as desired, for about fifteen minutes each time.

Counter-irritants like pain-balms or sprays can be used if desired. They work on the principle that if a fresh irritation is super-imposed upon an existing one (i.e., back pain), the nerve-endings (that were carrying the original pain impulses) get confused, resulting into pain-relief. They also cause a nervous reflex that leads to dilatation of small blood vessels, thereby helping in the removal of metabolic wastes accumulated in muscles.

"FOR HOW LONG SHOULD SUCH HOME TREATMENT BE CONTINUED ?" is a question you are surely going to ask. Well, eight to ten days' rest usually proves sufficient. Most backaches settle in about a week's time (or even earlier). If, during this period of eight to ten days, you have not got worse and yet have not recovered fully, you can as well consider continuing bed-rest for two to three weeks.

During this recommended 8–10 days' period, as your pain eases, you can gradually cut down upon the number of analgesic tablets you take each day.

When you are completely pain-free without a medicine, you can gradually resume physical activity to attain, step by step, the old level of work. However, for quite some days, refrain from undertaking physically demanding jobs. This advice to exercise caution is based upon the fact that though you are pain-free and feeling terrific, you may not quite be your old self. You may be having weak back muscles which might succumb again to even a trivial strain, as they did when you first suffered acute pain.

In our practice, we put our patient to the 'back fitness test' about a month after he or she has achieved complete freedom from pain. This test helps us to judge the condition of the key postural muscles, which if found weak or short, can be strengthened and reconditioned with simple exercises. Only when our patient fares very well in a repeat back fitness test, do we give him or her the green signal to abandon undue caution and resume all physical activity. The back fitness test, referred to here, has been fully described in the next chapter. Why don't you, too, take the test to find out how your back muscles measure up ?

Though we have advised you to manage your acute back pain on your own, there are times when you should take your back to a good doctor. Here is a list, in order of urgency, of all the circumstances that warrant medical intervention :

(1) You are having trouble urinating, especially getting the stream flowing.

(2) You have weakness in one or both legs that is getting worse.

(3) Your severe back – pain is preceded or accompanied by involuntary weight-loss or pain elsewhere in the body.

(4) Your severe back pain is accompanied by a fever that isn't due to an obvious cold.

(5) Your pain is very intense, and is getting worse no matter what you do.

(6) Along with backache, you have pain or swelling in other joints like fingers, wrists, elbows, hips, knees and ankles.

(7) You have had moderately severe back pain for an extended period (more than three or four weeks).

(8) You have had several episodes of severe backache and want to find out what is a actually going on in your back.

(9) Your back pain is severe and doesn't improve at all, even with eight to ten days' complete bed-rest.

(10) You have done the best you can and just can't stand it any longer.

Treatment of chronic back pain : Orthodox medicine, unfortunately, pays little attention to preventive back care, choosing to ignore its own preaching of 'Prevention is better than cure'. This is evident from the facts that (1) the incidence of backache in general population is tremendously high and (2) in cases of many back-patients, the problem becomes recurrent or chronic.

Chronic backache is a somewhat difficult problem to tackle. To make matters worse, management of chronic backache is a field full of confusion, contradictory opinions, unanswered questions, myriad therapies (orthodox as well as unorthodox) and, yes, some dubious practitioners. Indeed, the patient sometimes feels as though he is a wanderer in a medical and quasi-medical labyrinth.

Because of an indifference to recommending preventive measures and an absence of clear-cut principles of treatment, the poor patient suffering from chronic low back-pain gets on, what is called, the treatment treadmill. "X-rays are taken and, in almost 50 to 60 per cent of cases, depending upon how rigorously they are interpreted, they show structural defects or evidence of 'arthritis' that have been associated with 'instability' and pain in the spine (actually they are found with similar frequency in individuals without pain). The patient is hospitalised for several weeks of traction therapy, usually with a diagnosis of 'disc disease'. Consultations are arranged with orthopaedists, neurologists, neuro-surgeons and so on. Special X-rays and other diagnostic procedures are undertaken; nerve blocks and other types of injections may be tried. When these measures fail, surgery to correct the structural defect is usually advised. Repeated hospitalisation and surgery are not uncommon."

We have referred above to some modes of treatment for chronic back pain. Given below is an exhaustive list of diverse treatment procedures, variously employed : rest, medicines, physical therapy, immobilization of the back (with the help of belts, braces and corsets), massage, traction, local injections, manipulative measures like Chiropractic or Osteopathy (and the famous 'kicking' procedure frequently employed in our country !), Acupressure or Acupuncture, Magnet therapy and last but not the least, back – surgery. Most of these treatments are non-invasive and, therefore, relatively harmless. Local (spinal) injections and surgery are more drastic, invasive measures. If conversation flags at a party, you can get the talk flowing again by asking what you should do for your backache !

You may wonder how a single ailment has stimulated the evolution or application of so many therapies. But it is not surprising if we consider the fact that almost eight out of every ten persons suffer from backache at some or the other time during their lives, offering numerous chances for the trial of various treatments. A rarer disease would generate fewer opportunities to try out different treatments, and still fewer opportunities for them to catch on.

How, then, is a sufferer to find his way to the goal of cure through this maze of treatment ? Is any one treatment or particular treatment-combination more effective than others ? These questions are difficult to answer. In all fairness, we shall say that each of these therapies gives good benefits to some patients and not-so-good or no benefit to an almost equal number of other patients. Given below are objective and neutral descriptions of these therapies. You will see that we have described in slightly greater details, those therapies which can do no harm even if they do no good. One thing should be clearly understood : all these therapies can control or alleviate pain; but they can't prevent future recurrences of backache. In short, they should be undertaken strictly as short-term measures for pain-relief; but they are no substitutes for the preventive long-term action in the form of remedial exercises.

(1) Rest : Rest is the prime requirement for the alleviation of almost every disease or disorder. For back patients, it is more important since most backaches are due to a strain or spasm of the muscles and ligaments of the back. We would say that basically a back problem becomes chronic because the victim, through ignorance or sheer helplessness, chooses to disregard the warning signals (in the form of pain) and refuses to give his or her back the rest, which it legitimately deserves. A person with a sprained ankle would be able to see the swelling around his or her ankle and will be forced to rest. That would take weight off the ankle, leading to its healing. Injured back muscles or ligaments don't give rise to visible swelling. But that does not mean you should continue to move or undertake your routine activities. While you are sitting, standing or moving, you are forcing your back muscles to work because they must overcome gravity (which tends to pull you down). Unless you lie down and take weight off the spine, you won't allow the injured muscles, ligaments or joints of the back to heal properly.

Thus, even when your backache is chronic or not severe, it is a good idea to take complete bed-rest in a 'balanced pelvis' position for about a week. This, along with painkiller medicines and/or heat treatment, may prove sufficient to relieve pain.

(2) Medicines : Aspirin and paracetamol, as we have said earlier, are the most commonly used medicines for the treatment of back pain. Other more potent (and more toxic, too) pain relieving or anti-inflammatory medicines may be prescribed, if your doctor sees a need. Besides, if your backache is due to some specific disease (e.g., Paget's disease, gout, rheumatoid arthritis, etc.), you may require specific medicines for the same. All medicines, however, carry the risk of harmful side-effects. It is, therefore, desirable to take all medicines under the supervision of your doctor.

(3) Physical therapy : Physical therapy, usually given in special department of most hospitals, comprises chiefly of various forms of heat treatment, massage and gentle exercise, all basically directed at relieving pain. Heat relieves muscle spasm and brings about a dilatation of blood vessels, thereby working to remove waste products accumulated in muscles. Massage is much less popular today than it once was. Gentle massage is certainly soothing to the body as well as the soul. However, a back patient should never allow his back to be subjected to vigorous massage, especially at the hands of lay masseurs. Whether exercises should be started before the pain has completely disappeared (i.e., before the back has completely healed) is a controversial issue. **However, conditions like ankylosing spondylitis do call for regular gentle exercise because complete bed-rest leads to increasing stiffness and sometimes aggravates the condition.**

(4) Immobilization : A fractured limb is immobilized in a plaster cast to prevent motion of the broken bone and promote healing. Thus, plaster provides rest to the affected part.

The idea of immobilizing (and thereby resting) the entire spine with a whole-body plaster cast may in principle be correct. On practical application, however, such plaster casts, besides creating an unsightly appearance, are heavy, hot and uncomfortable.

A less drastic method consists of using corsets or braces. Such braces (commonly called back belts) do seem to improve overall function and performance. But in the long run they tend to produce joint-stiffness and muscle-weakness (since they take over, from the muscles, the work of stabilizing the spine). They should, therefore, be employed only as a short-term measure. In our practice, we have discovered that most people do not or cannot wear a brace tightly enough to obtain the maximum effect, i.e., to activate the hydraulic sac mechanism so that the lifting forces are distributed and the stress on the spine is reduced. Patients complain that a tightly bound brace causes difficulty in breathing and discomfort from perspiration, especially in summer. It thus, seems a no-win situation.

To summarize, we will say that if found comfortable and helpful, a back brace can be used for a short period. But its prolonged use should be avoided because it inactivates the muscles by taking over their work. Remember that muscles get stronger with use and weaker with disuse.

(5) Traction : Traction consists of pulling the upper and lower parts of the body in opposite directions with a view to reducing back pain, especially that produced by a 'slipped' disc. Two types of traction are in use, each type having an equal number of advocators and opponents. In one type, the traction is applied continuously for a prolonged period (say hours or days). In the other type, the spine is subjected to traction intermittently–pull, release, pull–for seconds or minutes.

Traction does seem to help some sufferers of backache. But how traction works is still a matter of conjecture. A number of speculations, hypotheses and theories have been propounded. But none of them seems convincing.

Opinions greatly vary about how much pull should be applied to the spine. Some doctors recommend that the spine be subjected to 40 pounds of force; others counsel 730 pounds ! Did you believe medicine is an exact science ?

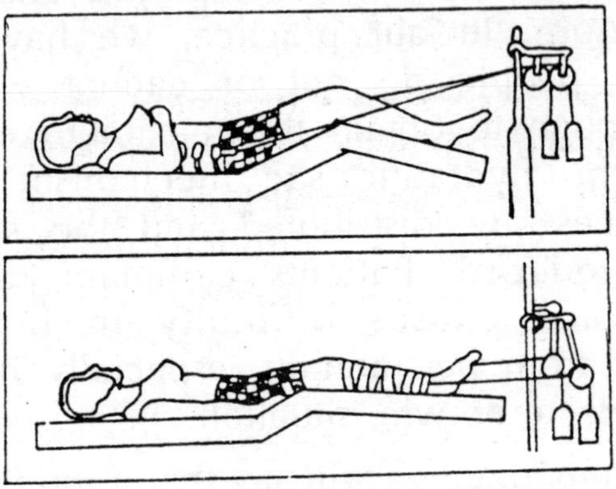

Fig. 5.5

Sadly, the beneficial effects of traction are short-lived. One study indicates that in some persons, traction aggravates back pain instead of relieving it. It is no wonder that traction is much less popular today than it once was.

(6) Spinal injections of medications : Local injections of pain-killing (anaesthetic) and/or anti-inflammatory medicines (steroids) have been tried, especially when the backache is due to a 'slipped' disc impinging upon a nerve-root. The results obtained have been inconsistent. Repeated injections may have to be resorted to.

This treatment carries some risk. Introduction of harmful micro-organisms along with the injection needle and development of infection around the site of injection are two possible complications. Consequences may vary from chills and fever to paralysis of the lower limb/s.

(7) Manipulation of the spine : Manipulation is a term used for physical treatment comprising of various types of pulls and thrusts upon the spine. There is little doubt that in some cases, spinal manipulation can, at least temporarily, ease backache with or without sciatica.

There are two schools of practitioners who employ spinal manipulation in the treatment of backache. On the one hand are orthopaedists and physical therapists; on the other hand are chiropractors and osteopaths. The difference between these two schools lies in their philosophy rather than application.

Orthopaedists consider manipulation solely a treatment that breaks down joint adhesions (thereby relieving stiffness) and reduces muscle spasm. For orthopaedists, spinal manipulation is just a minor part of the total programme of back-care.

Chiropractors and osteopaths believe that disease can be caused by interference or blockage of the nervous impulses coming out from the spine to the body's organs and limbs. According to them, such interference results out of partial displacement (subluxation) of one or more vertebrae with respect to other adjacent vertebrae. They, therefore, strive to readjust the various components of the spine through manipulation.

Various independent researchers as well as research institutions (notably the National Institute of Neurogical Diseases and Stroke, U. S. A.), following studies and evaluation, have commented on these manipulative sciences. The essence of their opinions has been given below :

"The concept of chiropractic subluxation (i.e., non-observable partial dislocation in the normal position of two adjacent vertebrae) remains a hypothesis yet to be proved scientifically. This has been one of the frustrating aspects........when one is correcting a 'subluxation' that cannot be perceived by independent scientific observers, it is difficult to convince those observers that the treatment is effective.......".

In other words, the question of the efficacy of spinal manipulation remains unsolved, since independent clinical and scientific observers remain skeptical of its unverified premises.

Yet, the fact remains that, spinal manipulation is a popular method of treatment in the West. In our country, most orthopaedists frown at the mention of spinal manipulation and there are very very few qualified chiropractors and osteopaths (though you may find throngs of lay manipulators at the Chowpatty sea-shore in Bombay !).

We think that the main point to keep in mind is that an accurate diagnosis of the back problem should be made before manipulation is undertaken. A chiropractic treatment, given without first diagnosing the problem, may provide some temporary relief from pain but may mask a serious condition that needs more specific treatment. Manipulation can be dangerous when certain disorders are causing the problem. For example, when backache is the result of a severe disc-herniation, manipulation may increase the pressure on and irritation of the nerve root making matters worse. Again, manipulation to the spine of a person with osteoporosis may result into a fracture of the thinning vertebra/e. In other words, disorders like acute disc herniation, spondylolisthesis, osteoporosis and other diseases must be ruled out before spinal manipulation is undertaken.

It is difficult to know or predict which or how many from among the 'safe' patients will benefit from spinal manipulation. We will just say that if you are going for spinal manipulation therapy (from an orthopaedist, a chiropractor or an osteopath), your back pain should be improving after three to six treatments. If it isn't or if it is getting worse, manipulation is obviously not working for you and the diagnosis must be reconsidered.

(8) Magnet therapy : Magnet therapy is a comparatively new mode of treatment, which utilises permanent magnets as healing tools. Reasonably strong magnets are placed in contact with (or adjacent to) the affected part of the body during treatment.

Supporters of Magnet therapy claim that the magnetic field (in the form of electro-magnetic waves) produces the following effects on the body :

(a) It brings about a dilatation of local blood vessels. The resultant increase in blood circulation facilitates the resolution of inflammation, if any.

(b) It gives rise to eddy currents in the blood, which produce warmth, thereby reducing muscle spasm and promoting muscle relaxation. The pain is thus relieved.

Magnet therapy is delivered to the back with the help of magnetic back belts (much like orthopaedic braces described earlier).

There is a lack of scientific research to validate the claims of the proponents of Magnet therapy. However, it remains a fact that some backache sufferers do experience profound pain-relief following the use of magnetic back belts. What has been said for corsets and braces is true for magnetic belts also—they should be used on a short-term basis to gain relief from pain. If used for prolonged periods, they will tend to further weaken the already weak back muscles.

Scientific research and clinical trials are being conducted in some countries (notably Japan and America) to determine the efficacy of Magnet therapy. Till the results of that research are available, we can only say that magnets certainly do no harm, even if they don't help.

(9) Acupressure : Acupressure is an Oriental therapy which strives to influence disordered body-parts by stimulating specific points on the skin. At present, it is used throughout the world, especially in the treatment of chronic or intractable pain.

Though doctors trained in orthodox medical schools are highly skeptical about its efficacy, it remains a fact that Acupressure does give profound pain-relief to a fair number of backache victims. Controlled experiments (conducted by the United States National Institutes of Health) to determine the effects of Acupressure on experimentally induced pain have revealed that the degree of pain-relief obtained was equal to that produced by a sizable dose of intramuscular narcotic analgesic, such as 10 mg of morphine sulphate. That the pain-relief was not psychological was proved by the fact that 'poor' hypnotic responders experienced as good relief as did 'good' hypnotic responders.

When confronted with the above facts, skeptics retort. "Even if one were to concede that Acupressure works, in what way, precisely, does it produce effects ?"

The same question is just as hard to answer when applied to time-tested, popular and very widely used medicines like aspirin and morphine. Little is known about how these or other pain-killer medicines work. It is known that they bring about some changes in the nervous system so that our perception of pain is altered. But the exact mechanism of these changes is still a mystery.

We have studied Acupressure from the viewpoint of modern neurology and neurophysiology. Our view, which agrees with that of a number of researchers, is that Acupressure produces its effects through the peripheral, autonomic and central nervous systems. There are many points of agreement between Acupressure and modern neurology. Many Acupressure points are located along nerve pathways with which any neurologist is familiar. Even then, the exact nature of the neural mechanism still remains a mystery. A number of theories have been propounded, notable among which are the 'gate control' theory and the 'neuro-humoral (endorphin)' theory. Though convincing, these theories do not explain all the observed effects of Acupressure.

We will say that Acupressure should be accepted on an empirical basis. That is, we can observe the effects, and we can reproduce the same effects again and again, reliably and repeatedly. Hence we can't help trusting those effects even though we are not certain about the underlying mechanism.

Our experience with a number of patients compels us to say unequivocally, "Acupressure undeniably works to relieve pain."

Acupressure enjoys some unique advantages : It is simple – even an illiterate person can employ it on his or her own body. It can be administered at any time, at any place and as often as necessary – you just can't overdose yourself (unlike medicines). It is harmless. Finally, it is inexpensive, in fact almost free.

A number of different Acupressure points are known to relieve back pain. Details about their location on the body and the method of their stimulation have been described in Appendix 1, at the end of this book.

(10) Back surgery : Here, at last comes the topic you were eagerly waiting to know about.

Surgery is the answer to only a tiny fraction of back problems in which a specific 'mechanical' derangement exists, for example, a severely herniated disc menacingly pressing against a spinal nerve (causing bladder dysfunction or increasing muscle-weakness in a leg) or a symptomatic spondylolisthesis (slipping of one vertebra over another) threatening an injury to the spinal cord. In these conditions, back surgery is inevitable and urgent. Even then, it is only one part of what will be a life-long process of back-care.

For other back-problems, surgery is elective, almost like cosmetic surgery. Its purpose is to improve the quality of life, not save your life or a limb. Such surgery should be contemplated only when—

(a) A specific abnormal process in the spine has been identified and documented,

(b) The abnormal condition has been present long enough to assume that nature and conservative measures are not going to cure it, and

(c) There is reasonable evidence that surgery will correct or eliminate the problem, thereby improving function.

Unfortunately, the results of back surgery are, more often than not, unsatisfactory. Figures of the success-rate of back-surgery performed in Indian hospitals are not available but, in the United States, surgery fails completely in about 20 per cent of cases, and three out of five patients continue to have distressing symptoms despite it. It is not uncommon to come across patients who have had two, three or even four operations and still have backaches. Indeed, such a situation is terribly disappointing and demoralizing for the poor patient.

And we have not yet mentioned other inherent risks associated with every operation : complications of anaesthesia, pneumonia, pulmonary embolism (a clot in a blood vessel of a lung) and serious infection of the operation-wound, to name a few.

In short, surgery is not the cure-all or panacea that back-patients dream of.

Yet, in their zeal to help, or labouring under an unrealistic belief in their powers (or capabilities), young surgeons, perhaps, do too much surgery on backache victims. That, incidentally, reminds us of a little story (our apologies to doctors who are reading this book) :

After bidding farewell to this good life, a woman finds herself outside the gates of the Heaven, about to have her credentials checked by Chitragupta. With her is a long line of prospective applicants, everyone on his or her best behaviour. Then along strolls a tall, stately figure in a white coat with a stethoscope around his neck. Without any hesitation, whatsoever, this self-possessed figure walks past everyone to the front of the line and enters the Heaven. "Who was that ?" people ask in hushed tones. "He was God," they are told. "But why the white coat and the stethoscope ?" people ask again. "Oh, he likes to play doctor sometimes," the answer comes back.

6. BACK FITNESS TESTS

The seven tests described in this chapter help you to determine if your back is strong, flexible and healthy or weak, stiff and unfit. They reveal whether or not your muscles can handle your weight and height. Any person can take these tests, regardless of age, sex, weight or height. **However, don't take them if you presently have even a slightest of back-pain.**

These tests are not the same ones that a doctor undertakes while examining your back for disease. The doctor who is looking for the range of movement, the muscle strength and reflexes usually conducts tests when the back is painful. These tests are different and are of little use in determining if your back is fit or unfit. On the other hand, tests described in this chapter will demonstrate how much muscle weakness and joint stiffness are contributing to your back problem or, if you have not had a problem so far, indicate what chances you stand of developing one in the future.

The tests also show whether your fitness level is on the decline. Are you in as good a shape as you used to be ? You like your car to be checked, tuned up or overhauled from time to time. How about your body ? Take the tests and see if your back is working as well as it did some years ago. Moreover, the tests are standardized and offer a comparative means of measurement — you can find out how your back compares with that of other people around you.

In the past, people who have suffered from back problems have not been told about or assessed regarding the condition of their backs. All anyone with a back problem could do was hope that no fresh problem will prop up in future. But the back-fitness tests described here will clearly show just what shape your back is in and, therefore, the level of stress it can withstand. In other words, the results of these tests may serve to reassure you that you have little to worry about; but more likely, given the way we live now, they will warn you that your back is vulnerable to injury and strain. Remember that the first muscles to deteriorate when we are unfit or do nothing to remain fit are the stomach and the back muscles.

The tests look quite easy but they are actually quite difficult when done correctly and with attention to detail. It is hard to believe that many persons score poorly while taking these tests. In fact, only about one out of ten persons can perform all the four tests at grade one, the excellent level. Persons who have suffered from back-pain earlier almost certainly fare poorly in these tests.

Remember that these seven tests are not exercises. If you don't do well when you take them, read the next chapter and learn what exercises you need to recondition your back.

Do these fitness tests lying down on an exercise mat or a firm matress but not hard floor. Make sure you are comfortable. Wear such clothes as allow free and easy movement. Preferable, strip down to your underclothes.

Test 1 : The forward bend

Aim : To determine the flexibility of the back.

Starting position : Stand in an erect, balanced position with arms raised above the head.

Procedure : Slowly and smoothly bend the trunk forward, bringing the arms down in an arc. Stoop forward as much as possible.

If the flexibility of your back is excellent, you shall be able to place your palms flat on the floor.

Other degrees of flexibility (or stiffness) have been shown in the pictures given below.

Starting position	Performance, rating and score			
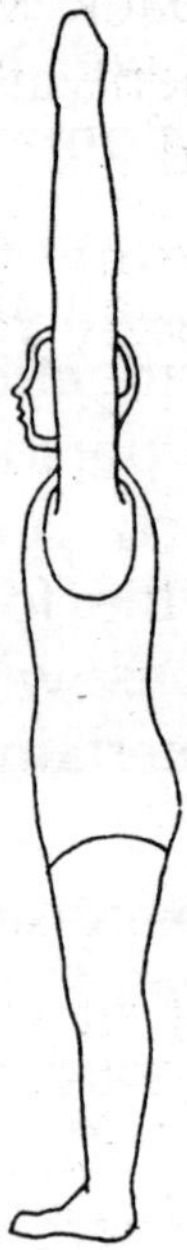	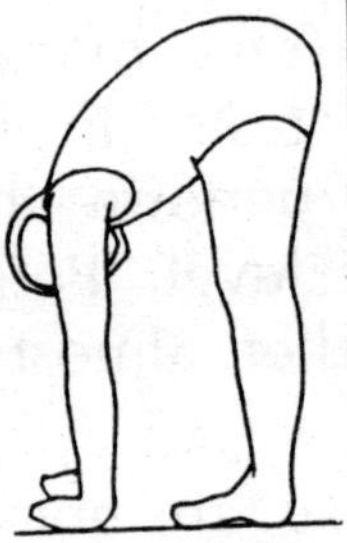	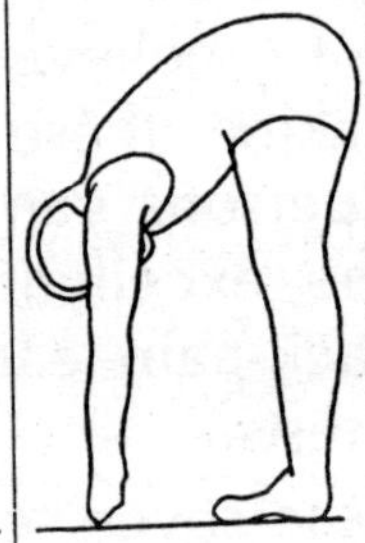	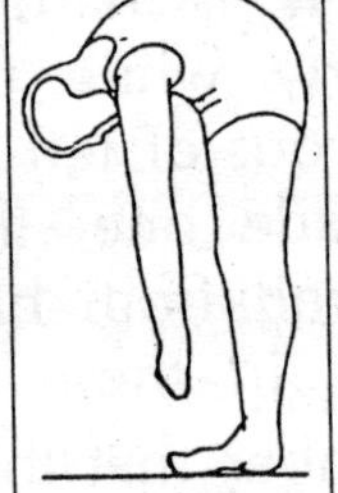	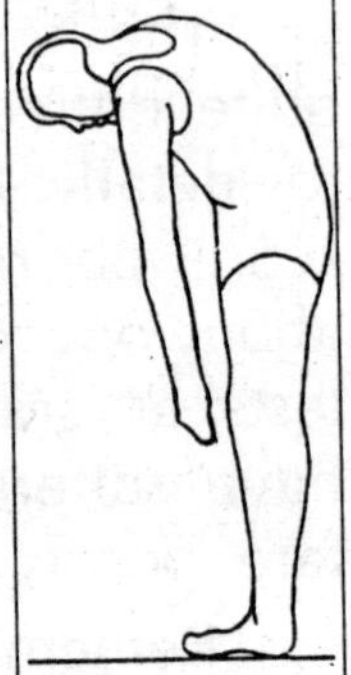
	Able to place palms flat on the floor-excellent back flexibility.	Able to touch the floor with finger tips-Good back flexibility.	Not able to touch the floor. However, palms go much below knee level. Fair back flexibility.	Not able to reach much below the knee level. Poor back-flexibility.
	SCORE : 4	SCORE : 3	SCORE : 2	SCORE : 1

Note : For a valid test, the effort must be slow and non-jerky. Jerking, in an effort to touch the floor forcibly, may sprain your back.

Conclusion : Not many persons fare excellent in this test, especially if they are fat, too tall, old or lead an entirely sedentary life. Similarly, persons who have had suffered from back problems earlier do not fare well in this test. A score of less than 3 is an indication that you need to take immediate active steps to regain back flexibility.

Test 2 : The bent knee sit-up

Aim : The primary aim of this test is to determine the flexibility of the back. Its secondary aim is to determine the strength of the abdominal muscles.

Starting position : Lie down on your back with hands interlocked behind the neck, knees bent at 45 degrees and the feet planted on the ground.

Procedure : (1) Without allowing your feet to get raised off the ground, sit up slowly and smoothly. If unable to sit up without your feet coming off the ground—

(2) Place your arms folded across your chest and try to sit up again. If unable to keep the feet planted on the ground—

(3) Extend your arms forward and once more try to sit up.

Starting Position	Performance	Rating and Score
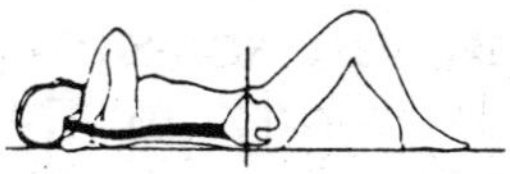	Able to sit up with knees bent and hands behind the neck. 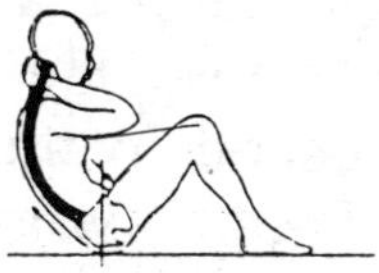	**Excellent** : Adequate spinal flexibility and stomach strength. SCORE : 4
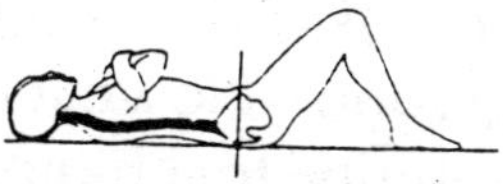	Able to sit up with knees bent and arms folded across the chest. 	**Good** : Need to improve stomach muscle strength. SCORE : 3

Starting Position	Performance	Rating and Score
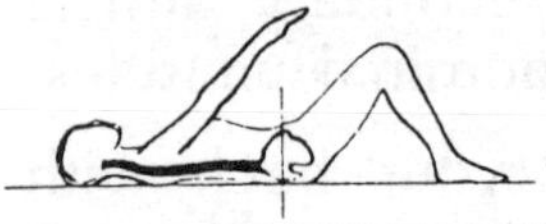	Able to sit up with knees bent and arms held out straight. 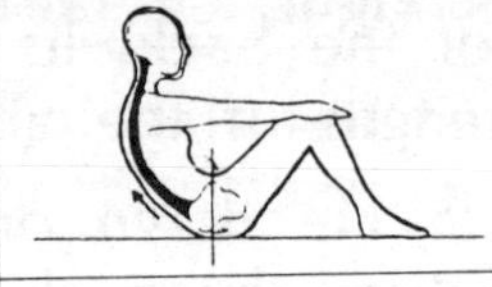	**Fair** : Need to improve spinal flexibility and stomach strength. SCORE : 2
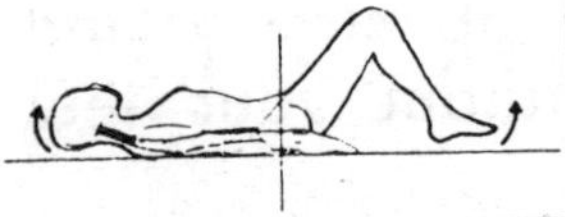	Unable to sit up with the knees bent.	**Poor** : Need a great deal of improvement in both strength and flexibility. SCORE : 1

Notes : (1) Do not raise your trunk with a jerk. This may aggravate a neck problem or sprain your back.

(2) Do not tuck your feet under something or have someone hold them down. This invalidates the test. It makes it easier to perform because it activates the leg muscles, which pull the back to a sitting position. Pulling yourself up in this way can also harm a weak back.

Conclusion : Many people are disappointed when they fail such a simple test. Flexibility of the back is more important to succeed in this test than are strong abdominal muscles. People who fare poorly in this test include :

(1) Old people,

(2) Muscular persons who have not paid attention to maintaining back-flexibility. They often feel that they fail this test because the weight of their trunk causes their feet to come off the ground. However, persons with flexible backs have an ability to change their centre of gravity, allowing them to sit up despite the heaviness of their trunk,

(3) Persons whose backs have been rendered stiff due to repeated back problems.

Test 3 : Bilateral straight leg raise (S.L.R.)

Aim : To determine the strength of abdominal muscles.

Starting position : Lie down on your back. Place your palms underneath the hollow of your back (i.e., between your lower back and the ground).

Procedure : (1) Eliminate the hollow of your back by contracting the abdominal and stomach muscles. Thus, hold your back tightly against your palms.

(2) Slowly and smoothly, raise both legs about one foot off the ground.

(3) Keep the legs raised for ten counts and then slowly return to the starting position.

(4) Throughout the procedure, keep the abdominal muscles contracted so as to keep the hollow of the back flattened.

Starting Position	Performance,	Rating and Score
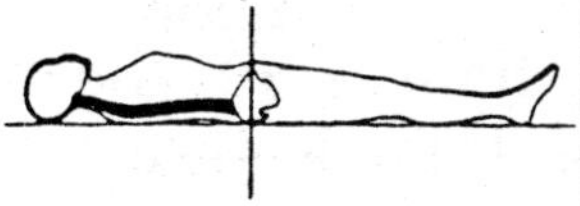	Able to keep the back flat while raising the legs for ten seconds. 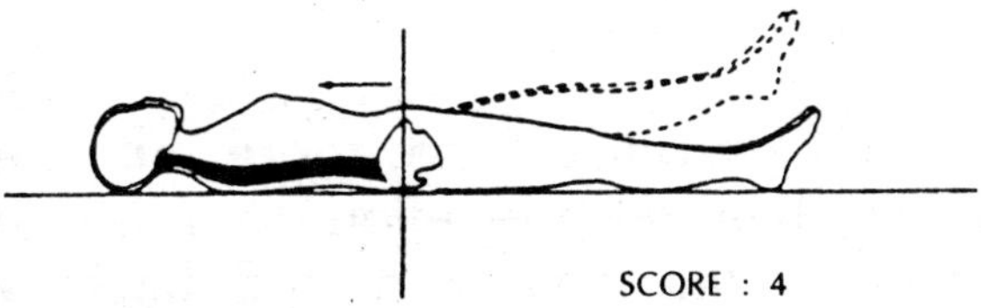	**Excellent** : Can demonstrate balanced pelvic position and hold it under extreme stress. SCORE : 4

Starting Position	Performance	Rating and Score
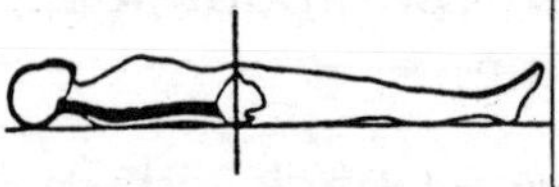	Able to raise the legs for several seconds, but the back curves part away through the test. 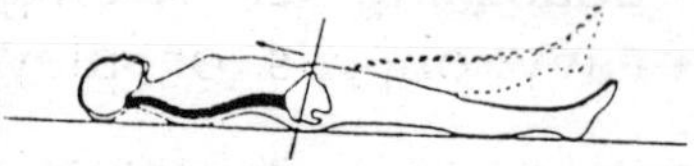	**Good** : Can demonstrate balances pelvic position, but need more stomach muscle strength and training to hold good posture under extreme stress. SCORE : 3
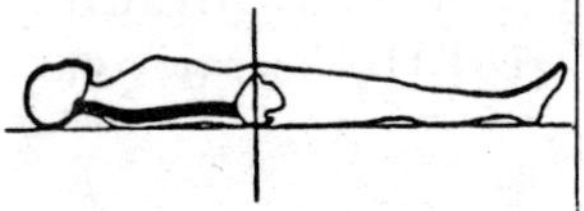	Able out lift the legs, but the back curves as soon as the legs are raised. 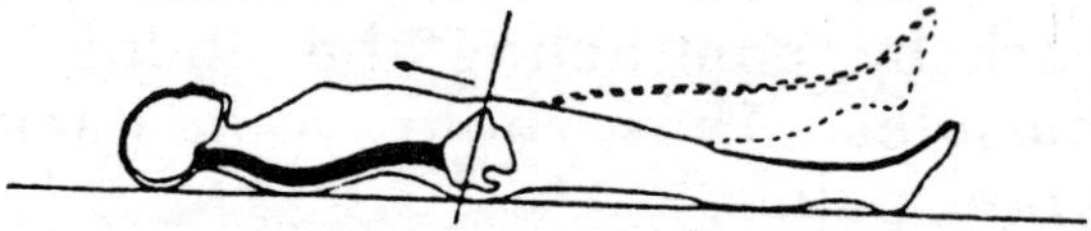	**Fair** : Need training in balanced pelvic position and increased stomach muscles strength. SCORE : 2
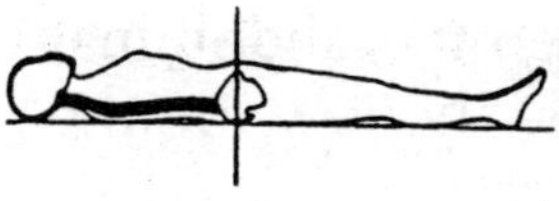	Unable to lift both legs but can lift one at a time. 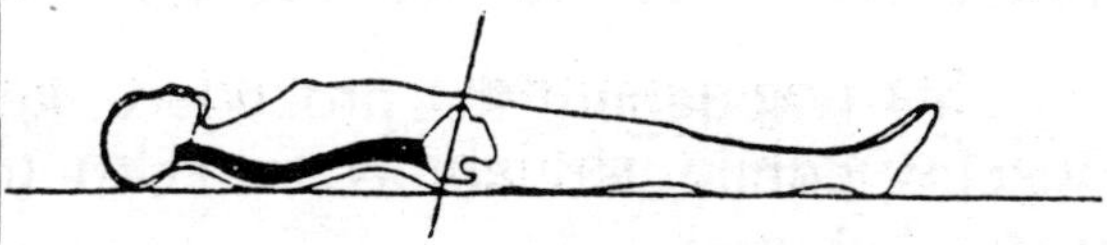	**Poor** : Need extensive training in balanced pelvic position and increased stomach muscles strength. SCORE : 1

Notes : (1) Raising the head off the ground renders the test easier and invalid.

(2) Lifting the legs too high also makes the test easier.

(3) Concentrate more on the hollow of the back than on the effort to raise the legs. It is the state of the hollow of the back, which determines the score.

Conclusion : (1) This test is comparatively easy and every person, irrespective of age or sex, should fare very well.

(2) It shows whether the abdominal muscles can hold the balanced pelvic position (by eliminating the hollow of the back) under stressful conditions e.g., while lifting heavy objects or playing sports.

(3) An inability to eliminate the hollow of the back is an indication of short (tight) hip flexor muscles, ascertained by the fact that you can flatten the hollow if you bend your knees.

(4) People who fare poorly in this test are not likely to do well in test 4.

Test 4 : The single leg knee-chest position

Aim : To determine the length and the flexibility of the hip-flexor (i.e., psoas) muscles, which prevent us from falling forward when we are standing.

Starting position : Lie down on the ground, with legs stretched straight out in front.

Procedure : (1) Bend your right leg toward the chest.

(2) Grasp the knee and force your thigh against your trunk.

(3) What is the position of your left leg ? Does it entirely lie on the ground ? Or is it partially or completely raised off the ground ?

(4) Return to the original position.

(5) Repeat the test with the left leg.

Starting Position	Performance,	Rating and Score
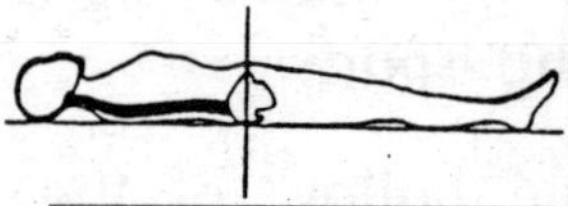	Able to bring your knee completely to chest and keep the other leg flat on the floor. 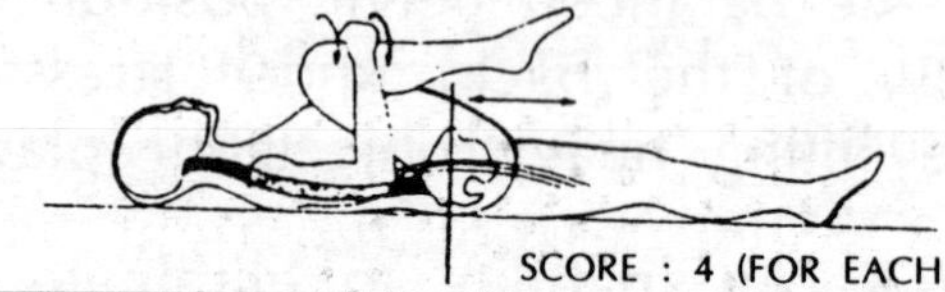	**Excellent** : Hip-flexors are of the proper length. SCORE : 4 (FOR EACH SIDE)
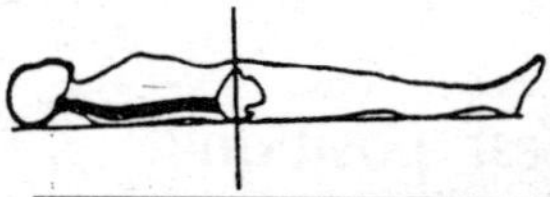	Able to bring your knee to your chest but the other leg lifts slightly off the floor. 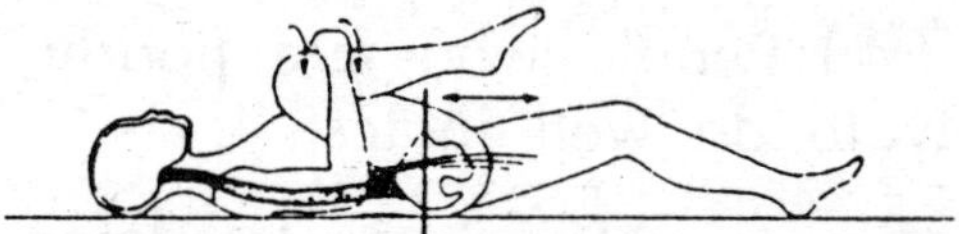	**Good** : Need to slightly stretch hip-flexors. SCORE : 3 (FOR EACH SIDE)
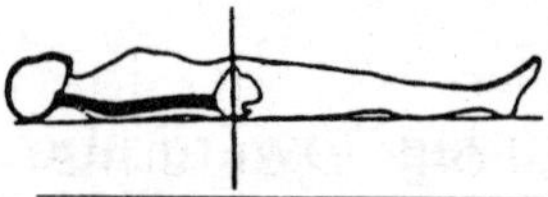	Leg lifts completely off the floor when your knee is pulled to your chest. 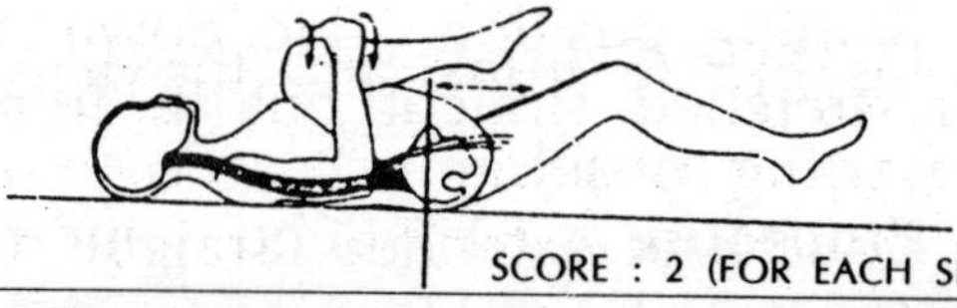	**Fair** : Need much improvement in hip-Flexors length. SCORE : 2 (FOR EACH SIDE)
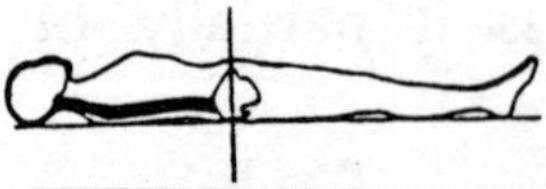	Leg files up into the air when your knee is held against your chest. 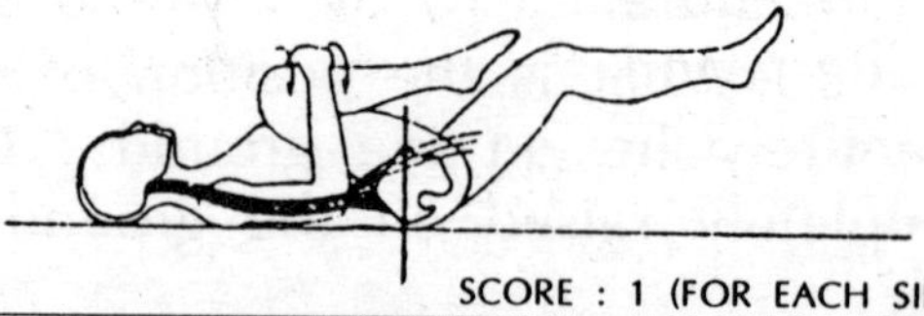	**Poor** : Inadequate length of hip-flexors—they need a great deal of stretching. SCORE : 1 (FOR EACH SIDE)

Notes : (1) The head must remain on the floor and the knee must be held snugly to the chest.

(2) The critical lifting off of the leg lying on the floor occurs during the last part of the test.

Conclusion : (1) Shortness of a muscle means weakness.

(2) Hip-flexor muscles come into play while standing erect, lifting, bending etc. and their shortness makes the back vulnerable to injury.

(3) Shortness of the right as well as the left hip-flexors is usually found in athletes. This condition may cause no problem during the prime of life; but if the abdominal muscles become weak later in life or a pot belly forms, there will be a tendency to backaches.

(4) One-sided shortening of the hip-flexors is usually associated with an injury to that side, causing pain down that leg. It is also associated with a weakness of the lateral muscles of that side, the test for which has been described next.

Test 5 : The lateral trunk lift

Aim : To determine the strength of the lateral muscles of the trunk and the legs.

Starting position : Lie down on your right side with your legs extended straight out. Fold your arms across your chest. Have somebody firmly hold your feet down by the ankles so that they do not come off the ground during the test.

Procedure : (1) Slowly and smoothly raise your shoulders and the trunk off the ground.

(2) Raise your shoulders up as far as possible and hold for ten counts.

(3) Slowly return to the starting position.

(4) Repeat, testing the other side of your body.

Starting Position	Performance, Rating and Score			
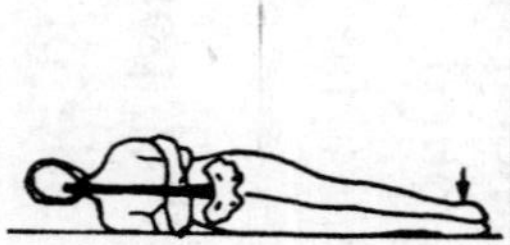	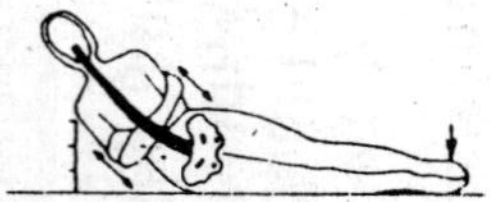	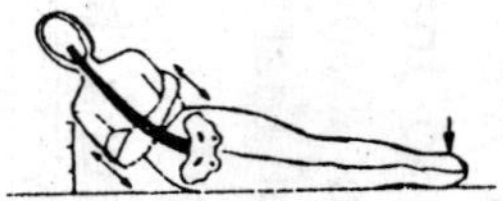		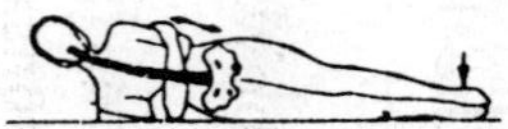
	Able to raise the upper body completely and hold for ten counts.	Able to raise the upper body up easily but cannot hold for ten counts.	Able to raise the upper body only a few inches and unable to hold.	Unable to raise the body off the floor.
	Excellent : Adequate lateral trunk muscles.	**Good** : Need to improve lateral trunk muscles.	**Fair** : Need improvement in lateral trunk muscles.	**Poor** : Need much improvement in lateral trunk muscles.
	SCORE : 4 (FOR EACH SIDE)	SCORE : 3 (FOR EACH SIDE)	SCORE : 2 (FOR EACH SIDE)	SCORE : 1 (FOR EACH SIDE)

Notes : (1) Perform the test slowly and smoothly. Raising the body with a sudden jerk invalidates this test.

(2) Do not use your elbow to push your body up.

(3) Your body must remain in one straight line during the entire test. Many persons bend their bodies forward or backward, thereby bringing into play some other unwanted muscles.

Conclusion : (1) This test determines the strength of the lateral trunk and leg muscles which are critical for upright posture.

(2) People who experience undue fatigue or discomfort in the lower back after long walks, jogging or tasks involving forward bending (e.g., sweeping) may have weak lateral trunk muscles and, therefore, usually fare poorly in this test.

(3) A poor performance on just one side of the body usually correlates with past injury to that particular side.

Test 6 : The upper back raise

Aim : To determine the strength of upper back muscles.

Starting position : Lie down on your stomach, with arms extended above the head. Have someone hold your feet firmly down by the ankles.

Procedure : (1) Slowly and smoothly, raise your extended arms, the head and the trunk off the ground. Hold on for five counts. If unable to raise the body —

(2) Interlock the fingers behind your neck and raise your head and your trunk off the floor. Hold on for five counts. If unable to raise the body—

(3) Interlock the fingers behind your buttocks and then raise your head and your trunk off the floor. Hold on for five counts.

Starting Position	Performance	Rating and Score
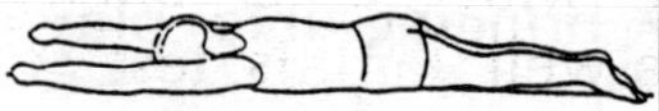	Able to life the body off the ground with arms extended above the head. 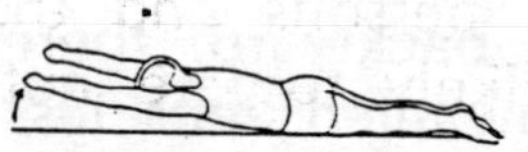	**Excellent** : The extensor muscles of the upper back in great shape. SCORE : 4
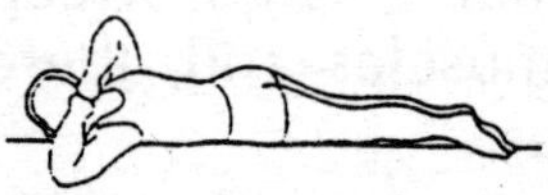	Able to lift the body off the ground with hands interlocked behind the neck. 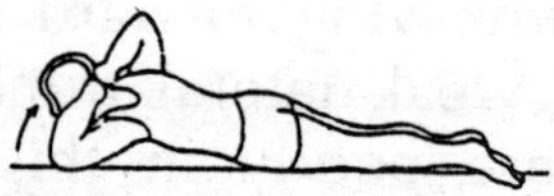	**Good** : The extensor muscles of the upper back strong but can be strengthened further. SCORE : 3
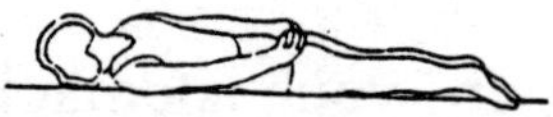	Able to lift the body off the ground with hands interlocked behind the buttocks. 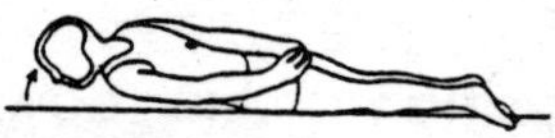	**Fair** : There is much scope for improvement. SCORE : 2
	Cannot lift the body off the ground. 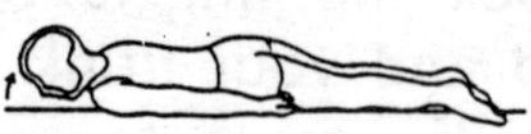	**Poor** : There is a desperate need to strengthen the extensor muscles of the back. SCORE : 1

Note : Perform the movement slowly and smoothly. A sudden jerk may cause back sprain or aggravate neck problems.

Conclusion : Most persons are likely to fare well in this test. Indeed, back-problems only rarely arise because of weak back muscles.

Fat or old persons and those with earlier back problems are likely to fare not-so-well in this test.

Test 7 : The double leg raise, lying on the stomach

Aim : To determine the strength of the lower back muscles.

Starting position : Lie down on your stomach, with the arms at the sides of your body and the palms tucked beneath the respective groins.

Procedure : (1) Slowly and smoothly, raise both the legs off the ground. Hold on for five counts.

(2) If unable to raise both the legs simultaneously, raise first the right leg and then the left leg. Hold on for ten counts each time.

Starting Position	Performance, Rating and Score	
	Able to raise both legs off the ground and hold on for five counts. 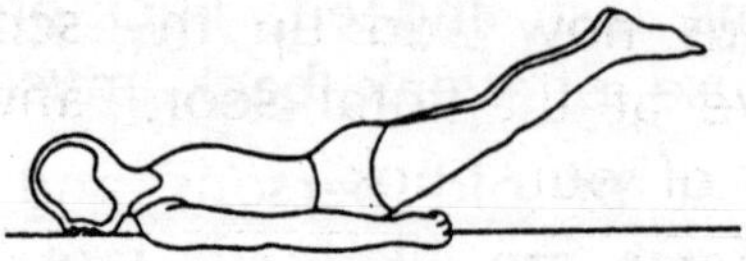	**Excellent** : Lower back muscles in great shape. SCORE : 4
	Able to raise the legs off the ground but unable to hold on. 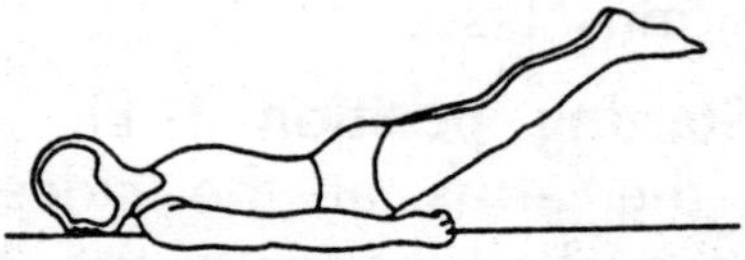	**Good** : Lower back muscles strong but can be further strengthened. SCORE : 3
	Able to raise only one leg at a time, which can then be held on for ten counts. 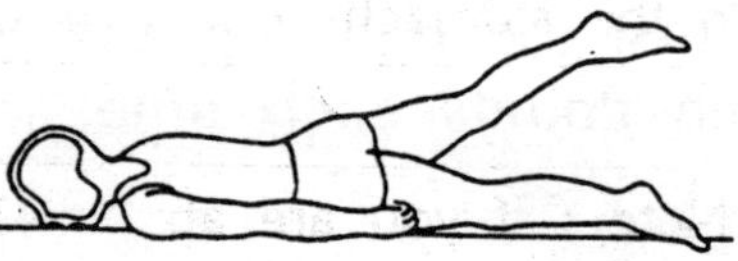	**Fair** : There is much scope for improvement SCORE : 2
	Able to raise only one leg at a time but unable to hold on. 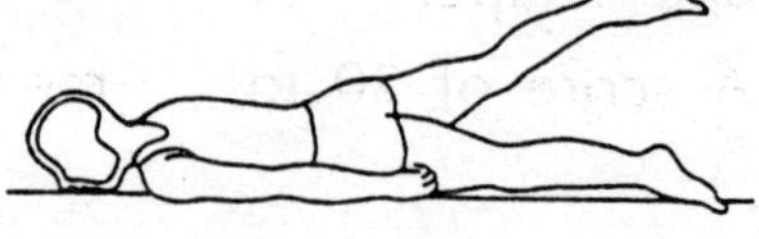	**Poor** : There is a desperate need for strengthening lower back muscles. SCORE : 1

Note : The movement should be smooth and slow. A sudden jerky movement may cause back sprain.

Conclusion : Most persons fare well in this test. Exceptions include very old or fat persons and those with a past history of back problems.

That brings us to an end of the back fitness tests. Let us now add up the scores of individual tests to arrive at the total score and hence judge the condition of our back.

Test		Score
1. The forward bend		
2. The bent knee sit–up		
3. Bilateral S.L.R.		
4. The single leg knee-chest position	Right side Left side	
5. The lateral trunk lift	Right side Left side	
6. The upper back raise		
7. The double leg raise, lying on the stomach		
	Total :	

Note : If you are above 45, add 4 to your total score.

A score of 35 to 40 means your back is in an excellent shape.

A score of 30 to 34 means your back is in an average shape.

A score of 20 to 29 means your back is in just a satisfactory shape.

A score of 10 to 19 means your back is in a poor shape.

These tests show how fit or unfit your back is. If your performance has been less than excellent, you have got some work to do to prevent back problems. Even if you have fared well, you will have to do some maintenance exercises to stay fit. Muscles which are not used waste away quickly.

Chapter 7 will show you which exercises will help your particular back weaknesses.

Chapter 8 will enlighten you about the simple exercises which will enable you to keep fit and, therefore, prevent back-problems for ever.

7. EXERCISES TO STRENGTHEN THE WEAK BACK

Congratulations if you scored well in all the seven back fitness tests. Chances are, however, that you didn't. But don't get depressed. Eight out of ten people who take these tests discover that their backs are not in good shape. A sedentary life-style and a disinclination to regular physical exercise have taken their toll : most of us have lengthened and flabby abdominal muscles, shortened hip-flexor (especially psoas) muscles and weak muscles at the sides of the trunk.

In chapter 2, it was explained that muscles work best at specific lengths. The stability and the efficiency of our back is almost entirely dependent upon associated muscles. If these muscles are short or unduly long, the back is rendered prone or vulnerable to injury, spasm and pain. But don't panic; a few minutes of simple exercises each day will, in a few days, get the various back muscles into optimal working lengths and strengthen them, thereby eliminating chances of all back problems – trivial as well as serious.

Why do exercises benefit ? Because muscles follow the nature's law of 'use it or lose it'. 'That which is used develops; that which is not wastes away'. You will find this dictum at a number of places in this book. We just can't over-emphasize the value of regular exercise – not only for your back but also for your entire body. Strong muscles provide so magnificent a support to joints that symptoms (especially pain) of even advanced osteoarthritis are not allowed to manifest. That is precisely why sportsmen and athletes have little or no knee-pain in spite of severe osteoarthritis of the knees. It is a known fact that women with knee-pain due to osteoarthritis are advised to strengthen the thigh muscles, especially the quadriceps.

You must have realized that the only aim of the reconditioning exercise programme presented in this chapter is to restore the muscles associated with your back to their optimal working lengths at which protecting the back becomes their second nature. The programme is replete with easy and effective exercises that will strengthen weak muscles and lengthen short muscles.

As we are all aware, the biggest roadblock to an exercise programme is getting started. Newton's law of inertia applies not only to inanimate objects but living beings as well. We all have a number of excuses. Over the years, there is perhaps no excuse we have not heard of. Here are some examples :

"I have already had one attack of backache some months back. It almost paralysed me. Will exercises not precipitate a fresh attack ?"

"I have arthritis; how, then, could I exercise ?"

"I am too old."

"I just don't have the strength; even the smallest of tasks tires me."

"My work keeps me awake till late hours; I can't get up early enough to do exercises – I will be late for work."

"The long travel by local trains saps all my energy and spirits."

"Don't I get enough exercise running after buses and standing in almost endless queues ?"

Wrestlers, athletes and sportsmen (sportswomen too !) are hard to convince. "Whoever said I have weak muscles ?" they say, their eyes focussed on bulging biceps, while they conveniently ignore flabby bellies.

"Exercises are boring; I have no one to give me company."

"I just don't have the time."

The last two excuses, mentioned above, call for further elucidation.

That exercises are boring is, perhaps, true. But, then, lying flat in the bed with an incapacitating backache is more so. It is a pity that our backs can't be completely fixed up with miracle medicines, physiotherapy, operations or the newest and widely publicized gadget hitting the market.

The excuse of not finding time is also partly true, considering the present day fast and extremely competitive life, especially that of cities, giving little time to an unfortunate individual for himself. That, incidentally, reminds us of one of our friends, Jagdish

Shah, who is an executive in a big, multinational firm. We met at a marriage party. After the exchange of pleasantries, he casually informed us that his mother had to undergo back-surgery for a chronic back problem, but that she was still far from happy.

We had the buffet dinner together. We observed that after finishing the meal, he could not bend enough to put his empty plate in a tub kept on the ground. Obviously, his back was not sufficiently supple. On inquiry, he confessed that he occasionally had a stiff and uncomfortable back in the mornings. He, however, had a ready explanation to account for such experiences. "In sleep, my pillow slips away from beneath my head, disturbing my posture. I think those episodes of back-discomfort are insignificant," he said. We requested him not to discount such episodes and invited him to come, one day, to our clinic to take the back-fitness tests. We opined that after evaluating his back, we would be in a position to suggest remedial exercises.

"My work leaves me little time," he said. "I am on the go all the time. Rat-tat-tat-tat. If I don't put myself under pressure, I feel abnormal and guilty. I have to keep my boss happy. If I work hard, I might be given a promotion in preference to my senior colleagues. Thanks for your concern but I am too busy. I think, I give myself sufficient exercise by playing golf, badminton or cricket at the XYZ club on Sundays. Besides, a fortnight ago my company had sponsored a complete medical check-up for its employees and I was told, thereafter, by the eminent physician that I was in terrific shape."

That statement did to us what a bouncer from a West Indian fast bowler does to a rival batsman — it floored us. Half irritation and half pity left us speechless for a while. "We sincerely hope that you don't have a back problem in the future," we said, subtely hinting that despite his belief, he was a prime candidate for back problems.

Barely four months later, Jagdish was at our clinic, clutching at his low back, which was in acute pain. Our hearts were saddened at the thought that something unnecessary had happened. Such incidents highlight the inadequacy of 'periodic' medical. The underlying ideology, in fact, is at fault.

"We want to catch a disease early," researchers say.

"Why not prevent it in the first place ?" we ask.

A person certified hale and hearty on the basis of sphygmomanometric and electrocardiographic examinations may leave for the heavenly abode the very next day. The need of the day is to prevent a disease, instead of spending time, labour and money to treat it. In fact, diseases like high B. P., heart disease, diabetes and backache can be easily prevented. The moral to be derived from the true-life incident presented above is that the less time you give to your back now, the more you will have to give later on. And not all back ailments are necessarily curable. But back problems can be prevented. With a few exercises, we can enhance the reserve capacity of our backs to counteract that fall or slip in the factory (or the bathroom), that heavy load we are obliged to carry, that suddenly over-stretched muscle in the gymnasium or the tennis court.

The first step to overcoming inertia is to 'realize' that if you faired less than excellent in the back-fitness tests, your back badly needs remedial exercises.

The second step is to 'decide' that you want a healthy, pain-free back. The third step is to 'commit' to 10-15 minutes of exercises each day. 'God helps those who help themselves.'

There are, after all, a lot of advantages of regular exercise. You will be a happy observer as you notice your stomach gradually flattening and your looks changing to younger and sexier. Your back will feel so good that your whole approach to life will change for the better. You will exude confidence, experience energy and zeal bubbling inside your body and feel much less tired at the end of a tough day. And these benefits will start accruing in a surprisingly short time—perhaps within a fortnight. Since the exercises look and are simple and easy, many people are tempted to think they can't possibly make much difference. But we are sure they are going to change your life. Well, then, what are you waiting for ? Start right away.

You should understand and always remember that all exercises are to be performed maintaining the pelvis in the balanced position. The reason for it is that in this position your back virtually becomes immune to injury or pain. Besides, your muscles are at their strongest in this position, enabling you to accomplish an exercise with a lesser effort.

Although the spine should be held straight by keeping the pelvis balanced 24 hours a day, it is impossible for persons with weak and/or short back muscles. That is why bad posture cannot be changed overnight. Unless you are physically capable of holding your spine straight, even endless nagging to correct the posture is not going to help. But once you have conditioned the weak muscles, the principles of good posture can, and should be consciously applied. It is a mental as well as physical training process. We will say more about posture in chapter 9. Before that, let's take the first step towards our goal—let's learn the method of balancing the pelvis.

You can balance the pelvis in two ways :

(1) By bending the hips and kness, whether lying down, sitting or standing. This is called 'pelvic balancing by body-positioning.'

(2) By training the abdominal muscles to straighten the spine. This is called 'pelvic balancing by muscle-contraction.'

We have come to realize that some of our patients find it difficult to understand and learn pelvic balancing. We will show you three ways to achieve it. Perform these manoeuvres to understand and feel the balanced pelvic position as you learn it.

Balancing the pelvis while standing :

(1) Stand with your back and buttocks against a wall.

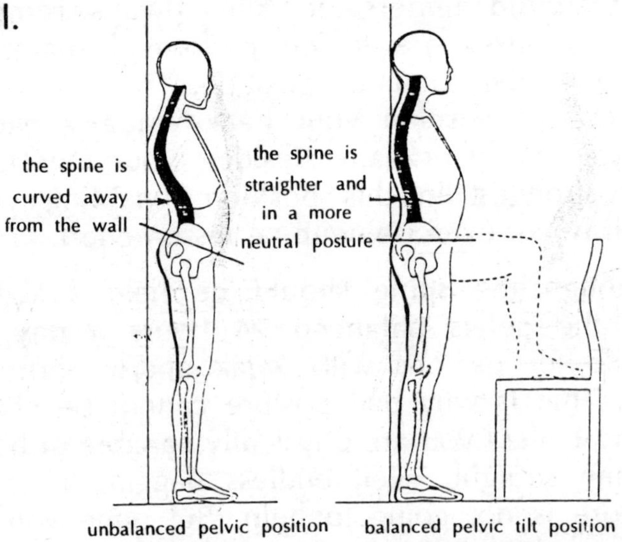

Feeling the pelvic tilt while standing

Fig. 7.1

(2) You will notice that your lower back has a hollow so that it lies away from the wall.

(3) Place one of your palms between the hollow of your back and the wall.

(4) Now place one foot on a small table lying in front of you.

(5) Note that your pelvis is tilted up and the hollow of your lower back has flattened bringing pressure on your interposed palm.

YOUR PELVIS HAS NOW BEEN BALANCED.

(6) Contract your abdominal muscles to prevent your lower back from arching again as you lift your leg off the table and lower it to the floor.

(7) Walk around the room holding this position.

Balancing the pelvis while sitting :

(1) Sit in a straight-backed chair.

(2) Keep your buttocks slightly away from the back of the chair.

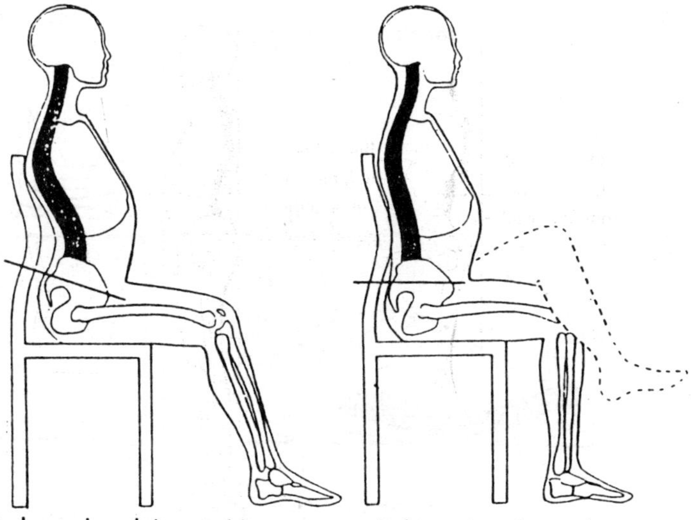

unbalanced pelvic position balanced pelvic tilt position

Feeling the pelvic tilt while sitting

Fig. 7.2

(3) Place one of your palms between the hollow of your lower back and the chair.

(4) Now cross one leg over the other.

(5) You will notice that your pelvis tilts up, flattening the hollow of the spine and, therefore, bringing pressure on your palm.

YOUR PELVIS HAS NOW BEEN BALANCED.

(6) Uncross the leg and you will find your back arching again. This can, however, be prevented by keeping the abdominal muscles contracted.

Balancing the pelvis while lying down :

(1) Lie down on the ground with your legs straight.

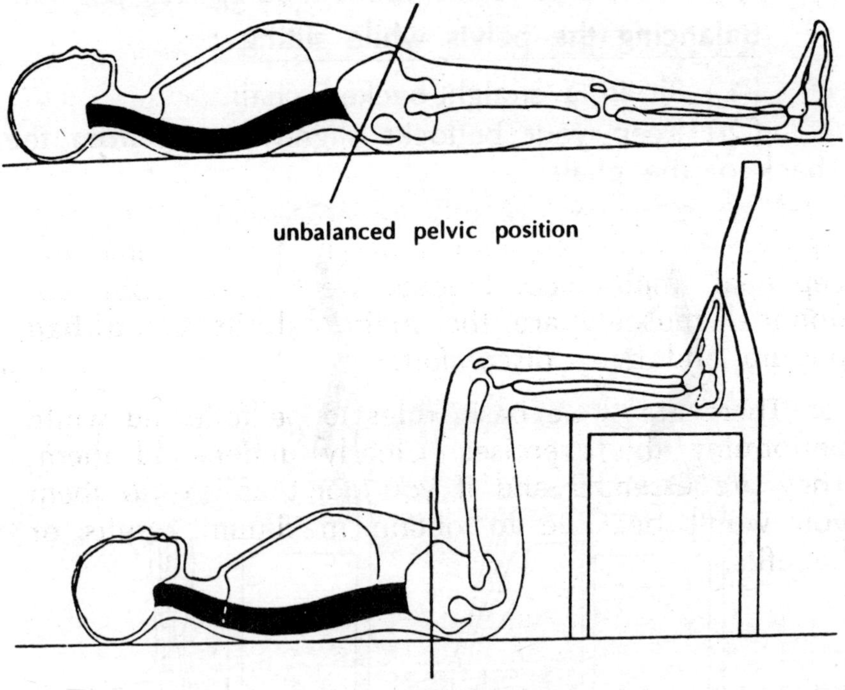

unbalanced pelvic position

balanced pelvic position

Feeling the pelvic tilt while lying down

Fig. 7.3

(2) Notice the hollow of your spine, which leaves a gap between the back and the floor.

(3) Place one of your palms underneath this hollow.

(4) Now bend your knees or place your legs on a small table.

(5) Feel the lower back straightening to press your palm to the ground.

YOUR PELVIS IS NOW BALANCED.

(6) Straighten your kness and take your legs down. You will notice your spine arching again. This can, however, be prevented by keeping the abdominal muscles contracted.

You must have noticed and realized that, in all these three positions, the tendency of the pelvis to tilt down again (i.e., the spine to arch again) can be checked by muscle-contraction. Since we cannot always stand or sit with one foot raised or sleep with legs elevated, strong abdominal muscles assume exceptional importance. Indeed, weak and flabby abdominal muscles are the main culprits for a bad posture and back discomfort.

There are some basic rules to be followed while performing the exercises. Clearly understand them. They are essential and if you don't adhere to them you won't be able to obtain maximum results or benefits.

(1) Set aside enough time every day (preferably at a fixed hour) for the exercises. Make that time a holy time. Ask your family members not to disturb you. Better still, coax them to join you. You will like your whole family to remain trouble-free. Take the phone off the hook.

(2) Don't start with the exercises immediately on rising in the morning. Your muscles might be too stiff then. Allow some time so that you limber up from a few routine activities.

(3) Do not be in a hurry to complete the exercises. The exercises are easy and simple and you might be tempted to rush through.

(4) Do only those exercises which are suggested for a particular week. Do not do advanced exercises that have been recommended later in the four-week programme.

(5) If an exercise causes undue discomfort or pain, discontinue it. Try it again after a few days.

(6) Don't strain by over-extending yourself.

(7) All movements should necessarily be smooth and non-jerky. Remember that a sudden jerk may strain a particular muscle.

(8) Wear loose or a minimum of clothes. Tight clothes hinder movements.

(9) If you are currently involved in jogging, tennis, badminton or any other sport or physical activity, give it up for four weeks. The reason for this is simple and compelling : the very physical activity you're doing outside the programme may be precipitating your back-discomfort. For example, jogging or running are known to shorten calf muscles, resulting into poor posture unless remedial stretching is simultaneously undertaken.

Every day, before you start with the exercises, you should perform certain movements which comprise the so called 'warm-up'.

Please do not skip the warm-up movements. They have a number of uses, viz. :

(1) They help in loosening the muscles and removing their rigidity.

(2) They prepare the muscles for exercises.

(3) They increase the blood circulation of the muscles rendering them warm. This is very important because cold muscles are vulnerable to sprains and injury.

(4) They reduce the possibility of post-exercise pain in muscles and joints.

(5) They prepare the lungs and the heart for the exercises.

WARM-UP 1 : ARM CIRCLES

(1) Stand, keeping a distance of two feet between your two feet.

(2) Move both your arms circularly in the following sequence :

Cross both arms across the front of your body feeling the stretch in your upper back muscles. Lift the arms above your head in an arc. Lower the arms behind your body feeling the stretch in your chest muscles.

(3) Repeat five to ten times.

(4) Then perform the movement in a reverse order, i.e., move your arms in smooth, continuous arcs from behind forwards.

Note : Move the arms slowly, correctly synchronizing their positions. Don't move them fast like a windmill.

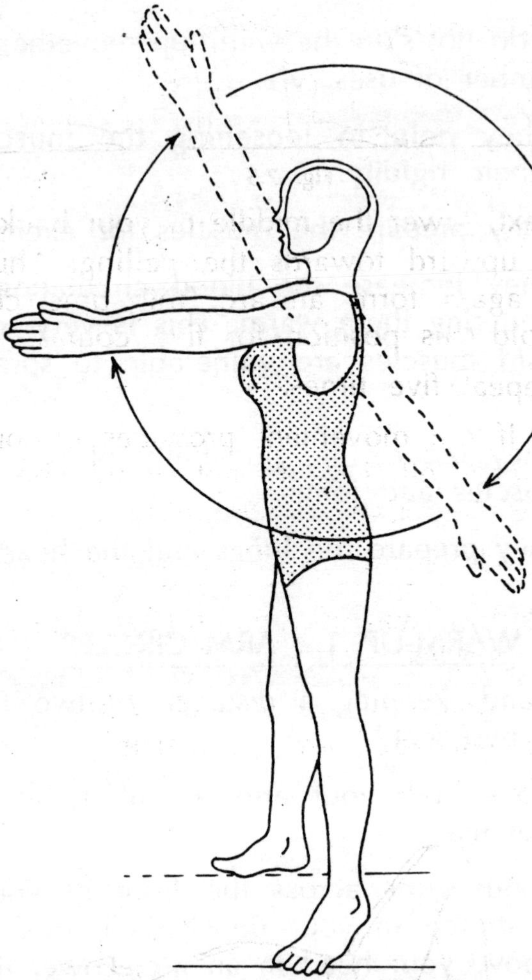

Fig. 7.4

WARM-UP 2 : MAD CAT

This movement relieves the back muscles of their tension and improves the mobility of the lower spine.

(1) Kneel on the ground on all the four limbs.

(2) Raise the middle of your back, bending your head downward towards the ground. Thus your spine will form an arc, convexity upward. Hold this position for five counts.

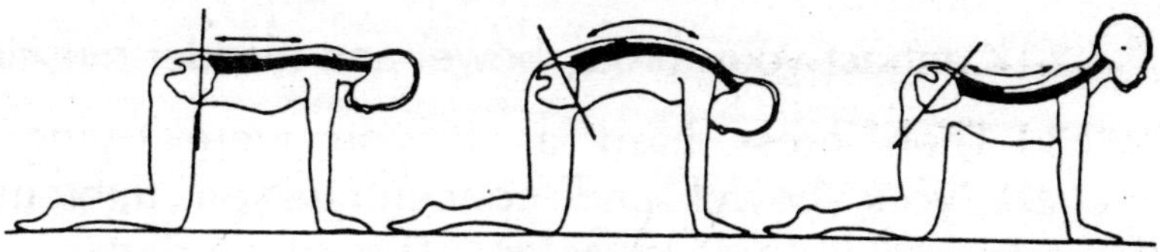

Fig. 7.5

(3) Next, lower the middle of your back, raising your head upward towards the ceiling. Thus, your spine will again form an arc, this time concavity upward. Hold this position for five counts.

(4) Repeat five times.

Note : If the movement produces discomfort in your back, ease off, i.e., do not stretch the back to full extremes. Gradually, work up to a full stretch.

WARM-UP 3 : ISOMETRIC ABDOMINALS

This action warms up and strengthens the abdominal muscles.

(1) Lie down on your back with knees bent at about 45 degrees and feet firmly planted on the ground.

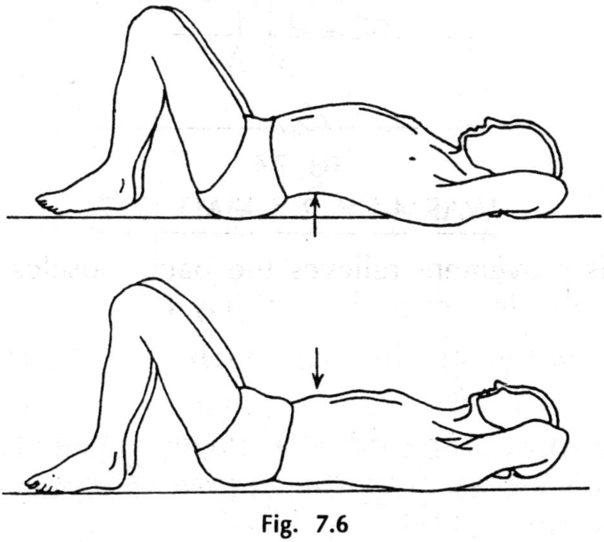

Fig. 7.6

(2) Contract your throat, bowel and bladder muscles.

(3) Then press hard as if you were trying to evacuate your bowel and concentrate on tightening all your abdominal muscles. This will flatten the hollow of your back.

(4) Hold this contraction for five counts.

(5) Repeat five times.

Note : Don't hold your breath as you contract the abdominal muscles.

WARM-UP 4 : LEG SLIDE

These movements are designed to release the tension of and relax the muscles of the middle and the lower back.

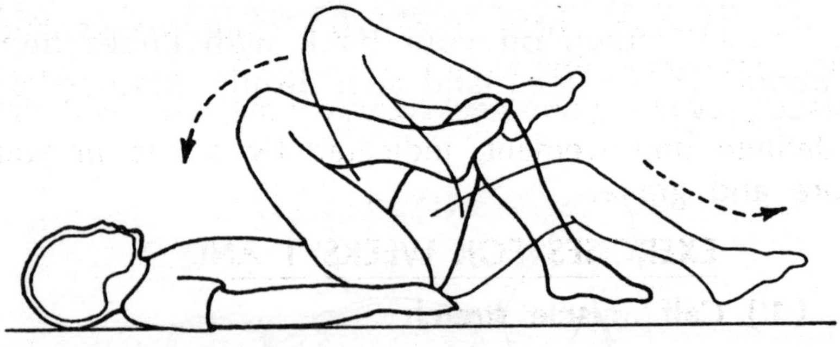

Fig. 7.7

(1) Lie down on your back with knees bent at about 45 degrees and feet firmly planted on the ground.

(2) Bring one knee up towards the chest, but not too far.

(3) Then return the foot to the ground sliding the heel all the way till the whole leg straightens out on the ground.

(4) Finally, bring this leg back to the starting position.

(5) Next, perform the entire movement with the other leg.

(6) Repeat five times with each leg.

Note : Don't bring the knee too close to the chest. If you do so, your buttocks lift off the ground, producing tension in your back. At this juncture, we want to release tension and not to create it.

With that you have completed the warm-up. You are now mentally and physically ready to undertake specific exercises to recondition your back. Perform these exercises regularly and conscientiously.

The exercises are common for men and women.

Two weeks, three weeks and four weeks after you commence the exercises, take the back fitness tests to revalue your back. Every time, you will find a definite improvement, indicated by a rise in your score and grade.

EXERCISES FOR WEEKS 1 AND 2

(1) Calf muscle stretch :

(1) Stand facing a wall, a little more than an arm's length away from it.

(2) Keep the feet together and the back and hips straight.

(3) Stretch your arms forward and place the palms flat on the wall.

(4) Lean towards the wall, bending your arms at the elbow until your forearms come in contact with the wall. Experience a stretch in your calf muscles.

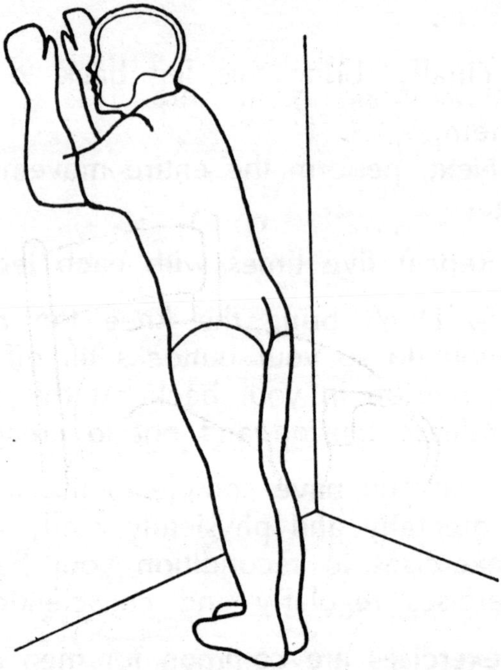

Fig. 7.8

(5) Hold this position for five counts.

(6) Using your arms, push your body back to the vertical position.

(7) Repeat five times during the first week and ten times during the second week.

Note : Make sure to keep your body straight. Do not bend at the waist. Keep your heels in contact with the ground all the time.

(2) Hamstrings and back stretch : This exercise is designed to stretch the back muscles and the muscles at the back of the thigh. These are key postural muscles. You will need a sturdy chair for this exercise.

(1) Sit forward in the chair so that part of your body-weight is borne by your legs. This helps to stabilize your body during the exercise. Keep your legs and feet apart on the ground because you are going to place your shoulders and arms between them.

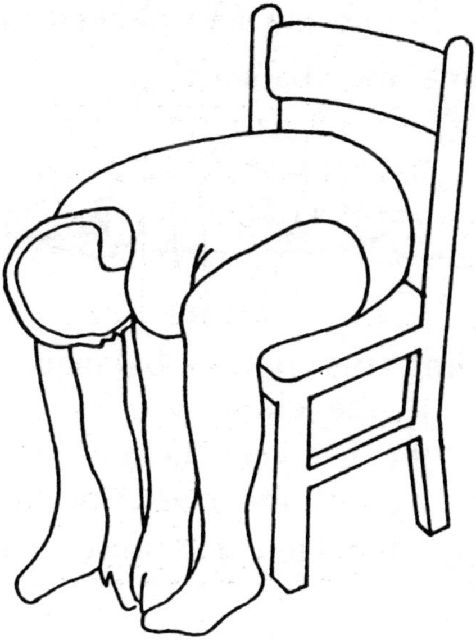

Fig. 7.9

(2) Slowly and smoothly bend forward, allowing your shoulders and arms to sag, between your knees and feet.

(3) Hang loose, as the saying goes, for five counts.

(4) Finally return, slowly and smoothly, to the sitting position and relax.

(5) Repeat three times during the first week and six times during the second week.

Note : Be sure that you don't jerk, bounce or force yourself downwards.

(3) Hip flexors stretch : This exercise is designed to stretch the muscles at the front of the hip and the thigh. These are key postural muscles which, when tight (shortened), pull the pelvis downwards and the lumbar spine forwards creating an excessive sway back.

(1) Lie down on your back with knees bent at about 45 degrees and the feet planted on the ground.

(2) Assume the 'balanced pelvis' position.

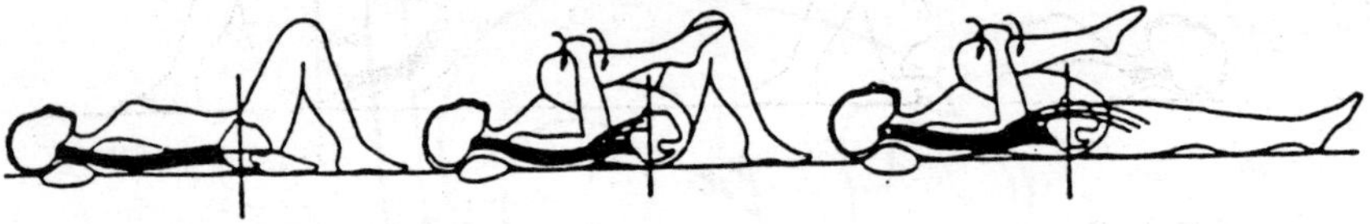

Fig. 7.10

(3) Holding the pelvic balance, slowly bring your left knee to the chest.

(4) Grasp the left knee below the knee-cap and press it tightly against the chest for five counts.

(5) Slowly straighten and lower the right leg to the growth.

(6) Experience the front hip muscles of the right leg being stretched.

(7) Release the left leg and return it slowly to the starting position.

(8) Release the pelvic balance.

(9) Next perform the exercise with the positions of the legs reversed.

(10) Repeat three times during the first week and six times during the second week.

Note : Refrain from aggressive stretching or bouncing. It can cause discomfort or pain.

(4) Bent leg sit-up : This exercise is designed to strengthen your abdominal muscles, the weakness of which plays a major role in the development of poor posture. You also get a practice in balancing the pelvis.

(1) Lie down on your back with knees bent at about 45 degrees and feet firmly planted on the ground.

(2) Assume the 'balanced pelvis' position.

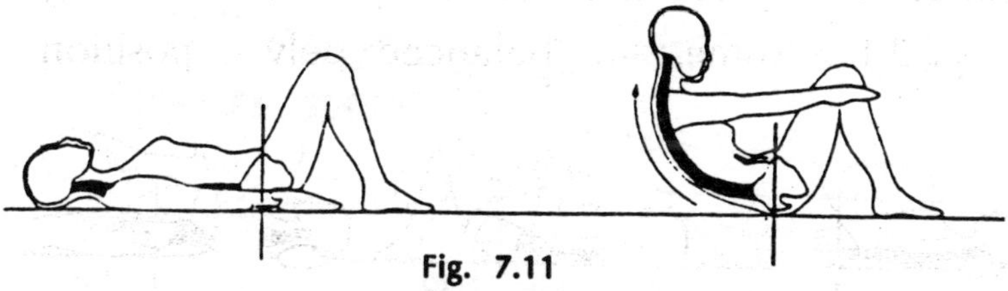

Fig. 7.11

(3) Extending the arms forwards, gradually raise the head, shoulders and the upper back off the ground, not allowing your feet to come off the ground. If your feet come off the ground, you are raising your body up too far.

(4) Immediately but slowly return to the starting position.

(5) Release the pelvic balance.

(6) Repeat five times.

Notes : (1) During the second week, maintain the raised position of your trunk for five to ten counts.

(2) Tuck your chin in while doing this exercise. Jerking the head aggressively may cause discomfort or pain in the neck. Curl up slowly and smoothly. If you try to come up too fast or with jerk, you may precipitate back discomfort.

(5) Lateral leg lift : This exercise is designed to strengthen the lateral trunk and thigh muscles. Weakness of these muscles makes them prone to sprains and injury.

(1) Lie down on your left side with your left arm supporting your head and the right palm placed on the ground in front of the chest to balance the body. Ensure that your trunk and the legs lie in one straight line.

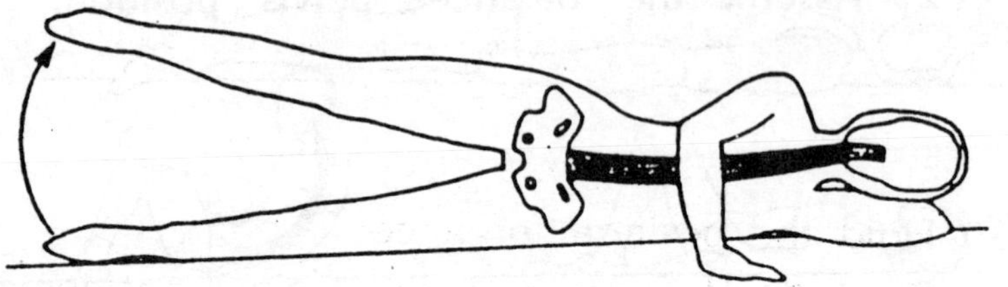

Fig. 7.12

(2) Assume the 'balanced pelvis' position.

(3) Raise the upper (right) leg by about a foot and a half.

(4) Without pausing, slowly return the leg to the original position. Release the pelvic balance for a while to rest.

(5) Repeat six times.

(6) Next, turn over to the right side and perform the exercise six times with the left leg.

Notes : (1) Do not allow your body to twist or bend forward or backward as you lift the leg. Do not jerk your leg up. The movement should be slow and smooth.

(2) In the second week, after raising a leg, hold its position for five to ten counts.

(6) Straight leg raising lying prone : This exercise is designed to strengthen the muscles of the lower back and the buttocks.

(1) Lie down on your stomach with arms at the sides of the body.

(2) Slowly raise the entire left leg by six inches.

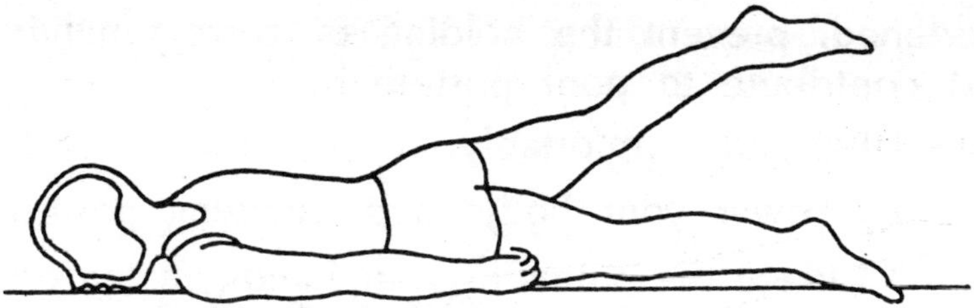

Fig. 7.13

(3) Hold the position for a count of five.

(4) Bring the leg down to its original position.

(5) Next raise the right leg by six inches.

(6) Following a five count hold, bring it down.

(7) In the first week, repeat five times with each leg. In the second week, repeat ten times with each leg.

Note : Perform the movement slowly and smoothly. Do not raise a leg more than recommended.

At the end of the second week, take the back fitness tests again. If you have performed the exercises regularly and religiously (paying attention to details), you are bound to find an enhancement of your grade. You are now ready to take on the more challenging exercises of the third week.

If, however, you are an exception and your grade is not seen to improve, perform the 'second week' exercises twice during the next week. That should do the trick.

EXERCISES FOR WEEK 3

Note : Before starting these exercises, 'warm up' your muscles each day as suggested earlier in this chapter.

(1) Racer stretch : This exercise is designed to stretch the calf muscles as well as hip flexor muscles. Both of these are key postural muscles which, when shortened, prevent the holding of correct pelvic tilt and contribute to poor posture.

(1) Stand comfortably.

(2) Lower your body to a squatting position.

(3) Place the palms of your hands on the ground on either side of your feet.

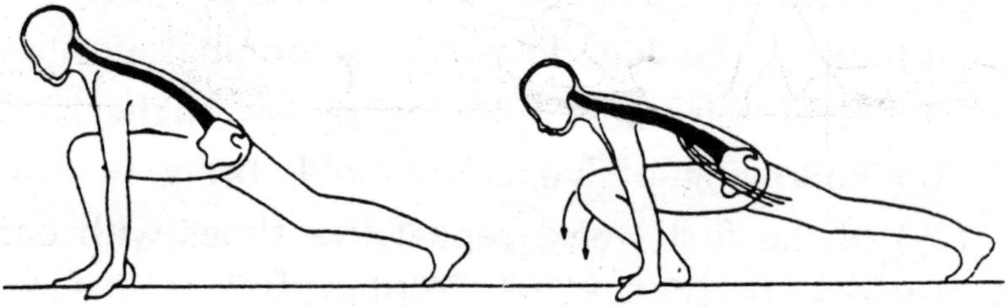

Fig. 7.14

(4) Extend your right leg backward as far as possible keeping the left foot flat on the ground.

(5) Allow the weight of your trunk to rest heavily on the left knee.

(6) Feel both calf muscles and the right groin muscles stretch as your body is carried down and forward by gravity.

(7) Hold for a count of ten. Then relax.

(8) Repeat five times.

Perform this stretching five times more after reversing the positions of the legs.

Note : Make sure that your trunk is supported by the thigh and the leg so that your back is not strained.

(2) Hip flexor stretch : This exercise is designed to stretch further the muscles at the front of your hips and thighs.

(1) Lie down on your back with the knees bent at about 45 degrees and feet flat on the ground.

(2) Assume the 'balanced pelvis' position and hold it.

(3) Bring one knee to your chest, grasp it just below the knee-cap and press it firmly against the chest.

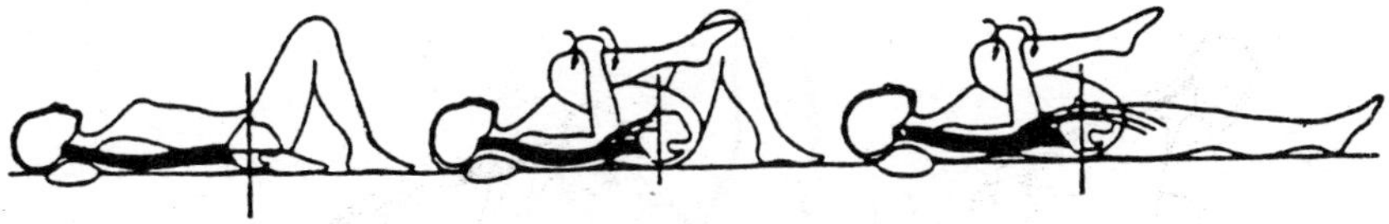

Fig. 7.15

(4) Extend (straighten) the other leg and pull it downward in an effort to bring its entire under-surface in contact with the ground. Hold for a count of ten.

(5) You will feel a stretch in the groin of the straight leg.

(6) Return the leg back to the original position.

(7) Release the grasped knee, allowing it, too, to return to the original position.

(8) Relax the pelvic balance for a while.

(9) Next perform the movement reversing the positions of the two legs.

(10) Repeat five times with each leg.

Note : This exercise may cause mild discomfort initially. But no pain should occur. If it does, that means you are pursuing the exercise too aggressively. Ease off and proceed more gradually.

(3) Hamstrings stretch : This exercise is designed to stretch the muscles at the back of your thighs.

(1) Lie down on your back with knees bent at about 45 degrees and the feet planted on the ground.

(2) Assume the 'balanced pelvis' position and hold it.

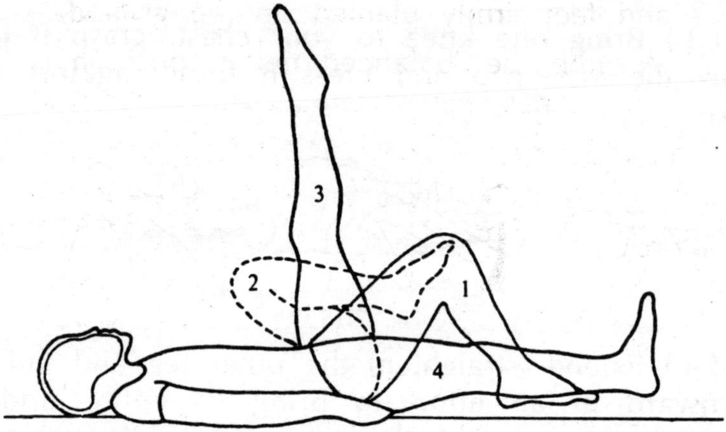

Fig. 7.16

(3) Bring one knee up towards the chest, but not too far.

(4) Next straighten the knee, to extend the leg in a straight line towards the ceiling. Experience a stretch at the back of the thigh.

(5) Hold this position for a count of five.

(6) Finally, lower this leg to the ground without bending it.

(7) Bring it back to the original (bent-knee) position. Release the pelvic balance for a while and rest.

(8) In the next round, perform these movements with the other leg.

(9) Repeat five times with each leg.

Note : Aim to bend the hip by 90 degrees as you extend the leg up towards the ceiling. However, do not pursue the exercise so vigorously as to cause discomfort or pain.

(4) Abdominal strengthening : This exercise is designed to strengthen the abdominal muscles and mobilize the lower back.

(1) Sit on the ground with knees bent at 45 degrees and feet firmly planted on the ground.

(2) Assume the 'balanced pelvis' position.

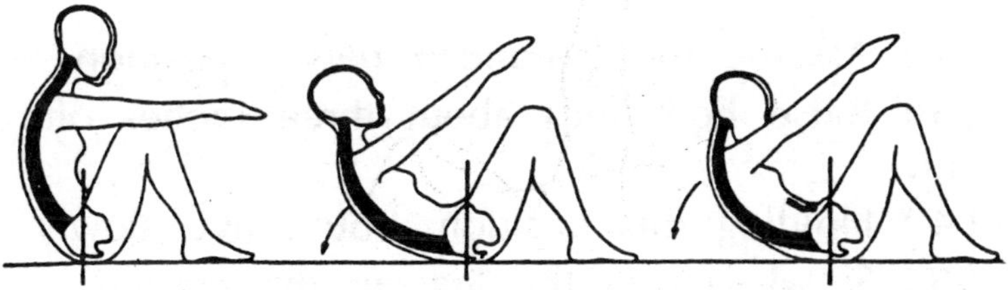

Fig. 7.17

(3) Slowly lower your back to the ground in such a way that vertebrae (from below upwards) come in contact of the ground one after the other.

Note : If your feet come off the ground during the exercise, roll backwards to the floor like a ball.

(4) Return to the original sitting position by pushing yourself up with your arms.

(5) Release the pelvic balance for a while and rest.

(6) Repeat the exercise five times.

Notes : (1) If your feet continue to come off the floor even after a few days, your lower spine is inflexible. It can be made more flexible by increasing the repetitions of the 'Mad Cat' movements of the warm-up.

(2) Don't forget to maintain pelvic balance when you lower your body from the sitting position.

(3) Do not tuck your feet underneath something to hold them down. This brings unwanted muscles into play and may harm a weak back.

(5) Lateral trunk muscles strengthening : This exercise is designed to strengthen the muscles at the sides of the trunk and the thighs.

(1) Lie down on your left side with the left arm supporting your head and the right palm placed on the ground in front of the chest to balance the body. Ensure that your trunk and the legs lie in one straight line.

(2) Assume the 'balanced pelvis' position.

(3) Raise both legs about three inches off the ground.

(4) Holding this position, count five slowly.

(5) Slowly return the legs to the ground.

(6) Perform this exercise five times.

(7) Repeat the entire procedure lying on the right side.

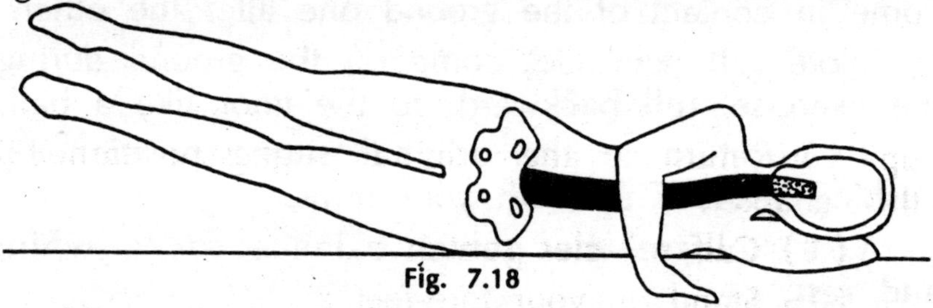

Fig. 7.18

Note : See to it that your trunk does not bend or twist forwards or backwards as you raise your legs. This will be more or less ensured if you maintain the pelvic balance.

(6) Raising both legs lying prone : This exercise is designed to strengthen the lower back and buttock muscles.

(1) Lie down on the ground on your stomach. With the arms by the sides, keep your palms flat underneath your respective groins.

(2) Slowly and smoothly raise both your legs simultaneously, about one foot off the floor.

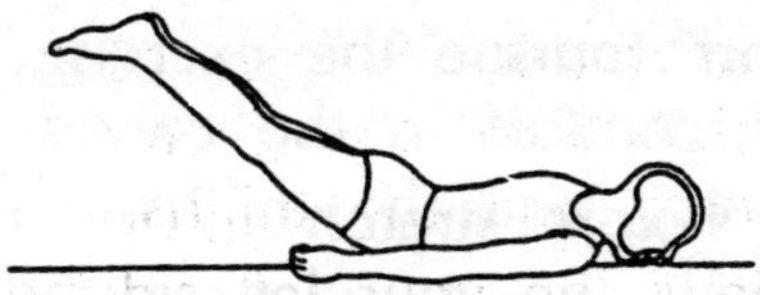

Fig. 7.19

(3) Hold this position for a count of five.

(4) Then slowly lower the legs to the ground.

(5) Repeat five times.

Note : Don't jerk your legs up. Don't raise them more than recommended. Otherwise, back discomfort may result.

At the end of the third week, take the back fitness test again. If you have been regular and diligent in performing the exercises, you shall discover an improvement in your grade. You are now ready to face the more challenging exercises of the fourth week.

EXERCISES FOR WEEK 4

Note : Before commencing these exercises, 'warm up' your muscles each day as suggested earlier in this chapter.

(1) Calf muscles stretch :

(1) Stand on your fore-feet at the edge of a stair. The back halves of your feet including the heels will remain free.

(2) Hold on to some object for support.

(3) Using your weight, make your body sag down so that your ankles are bent at an acute angle.

(4) Hold this position for a count of five.

(5) Repeat five times.

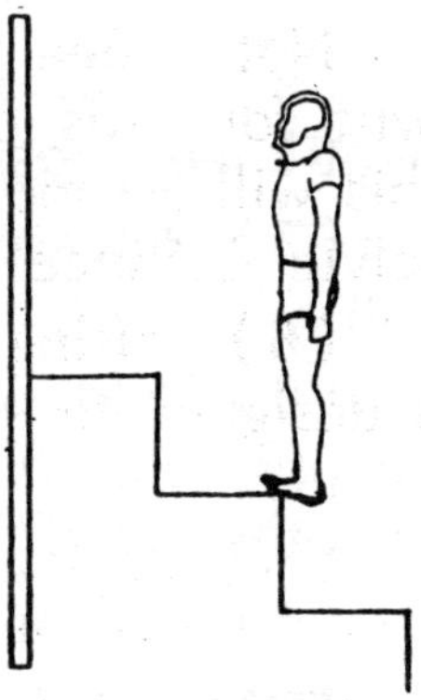

Fig. 7.20

Note : Don't pursue the exercise so aggressively as to cause discomfort in the calves.

(2) Hip flexors stretch : This exercise is designed to stretch the muscles at the front of your hips.

(1) Lie at the edge of a firm bed with knees bent at 45 degrees and feet flat on the bed.

(2) Assume the 'balanced pelvis' position.

(3) Bring one knee to the chest, grasp it firmly just below the knee-cap and press it against your chest.

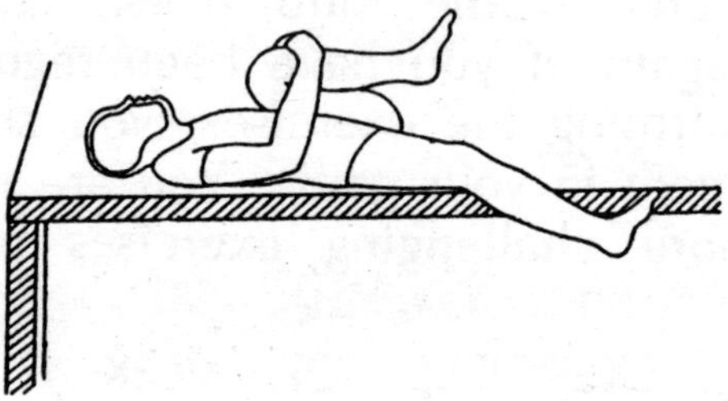

Fig. 7.21

(4) Slowly lower the other leg dangling it over the edge of the bed. Experience its hip-flexors being stretched fully.

(5) Hold this position for a count of five.

(6) Then return both the legs to the original (bent-knee) position.

(7) Release the pelvic balance for a while and rest.

(8) Next perform the entire procedure reversing the positions of the two legs (you will have to lie at the other edge of the bed).

(9) Repeat five times with each leg.

Notes : (1) The upper leg must be held tightly to the chest maintaining pelvic balance. Otherwise, the back will arch to a weak position.

(2) Don't pursue the exercise too vigorously. Aim for a gradual stretching over the week.

(3) Advanced hamstrings stretch : This exercise is designed to stretch the muscles of your lower back and those at the back of your thighs.

(1) Lie down on your back with knees bent at 45 degrees and the feet planted on the ground.

(2) Assume the 'balanced pelvis' position.

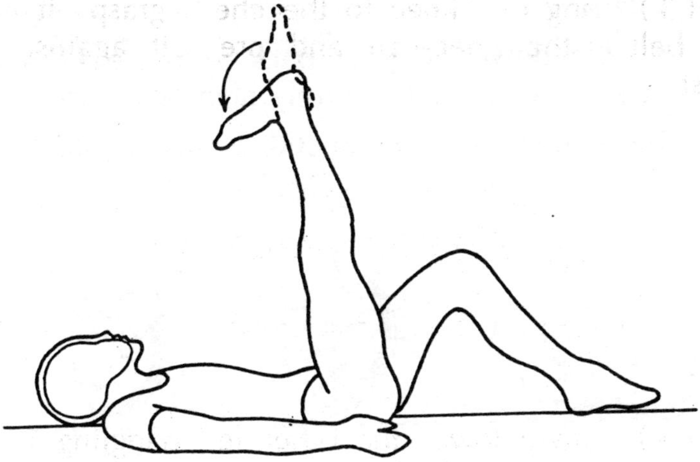

Fig. 7.22

(3) Bring one knee up towards the chest, but not too far.

(4) Now straighten the knee to extend the leg in a straight line towards the ceiling.

(5) Pull the foot down towards your head. Experience the hamstring muscles being stretched.

(6) Hold this position for a count of five.

(7) Next keeping the leg straight, lower it to the ground.

(8) Finally, bring it back to its original (bent-knee) position. Release the pelvic balance for a while and rest.

(9) Now, perform these movements with the other leg.

(10) Repeat five times with each leg.

Note : Move the leg slowly and smoothly. Do not pursue the exercise so vigorously as to cause discomfort.

(4) Advanced abdominal strengthening : This exercise is designed to strengthen the muscles of your abdomen.

(1) Lie down on your back with the kness bent at 45 degrees and the feet firmly planted on the ground.

(2) Assume the 'balanced pelvis' position.

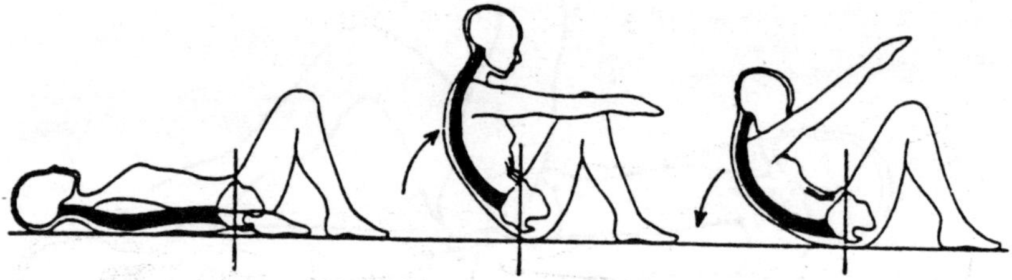

Fig. 7.23

(3) Extend your arms in front of your body.

(4) Slowly and smoothly rise to a sitting position, not allowing your legs to come off the ground.

(5) Then slowly and carefully lower your body back to the ground such that the vertebrae (from below upwards) come in contact with the ground one after another. Keep the chin tucked in towards the chest.

(6) Release the pelvic balance for a while and rest.

(7) Repeat the exercise five times.

Notes : (1) Do not jerk your body up.

(2) Don't tuck your feet underneath something during the exercise. That will exercise wrong muscles.

(3) The exercise becomes more challenging if you keep your arms folded across your chest or behind your neck.

(5) Lateral leg lift : This exercise is designed to strengthen the muscles at the sides of your trunk and your legs.

(1) Lie down on your left side with your left hand supporting your head and the right hand placed flat on the ground to support and balance your body.

(2) Ensure that your trunk and legs remain in one straight line.

(3) Assume the 'balanced pelvis' position.

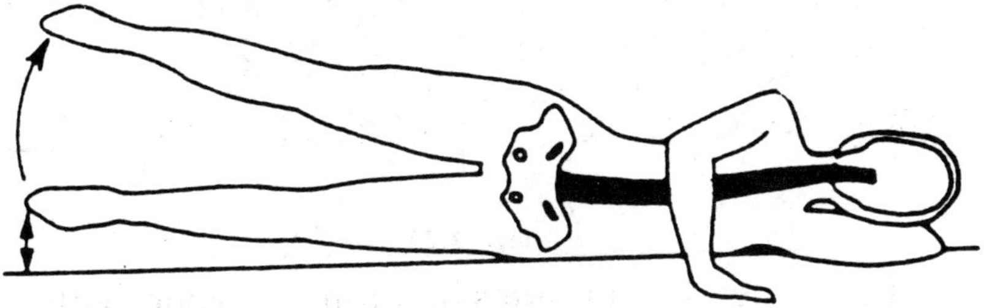

Fig. 7.24

(4) Raise both legs, about an inch or two off the ground.

(5) Holding this position, slowly raise the upper leg about a foot further up towards the ceiling.

(6) Slowly return the upper leg to the lower one.

(7) Repeat five times.

(8) Then turn over to your right side and perform the exercise five times more.

Note : See to it that your trunk and legs don't bend or twist forwards or backwards. This will be, more or less, ensured if you maintain the pelvic balance.

(6) Back muscles strengthening : This exercise is designed to strengthen the muscles of your buttocks and the entire back.

(1) Lie down on your stomach with arms extended above your head.

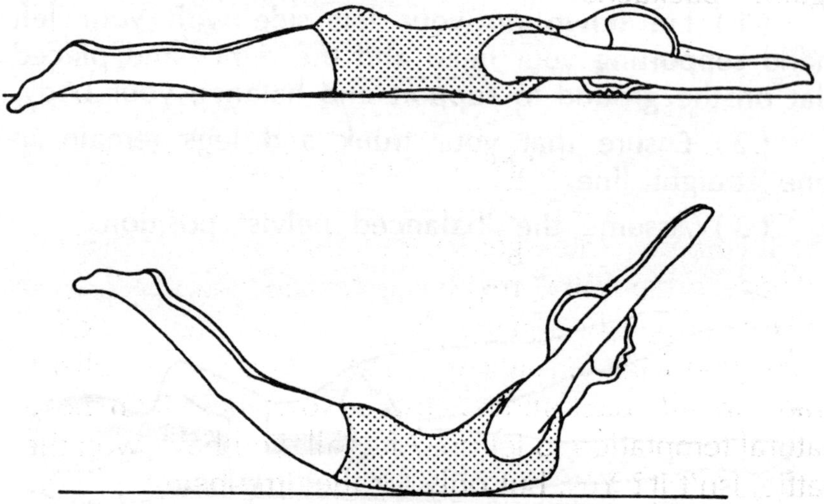

Fig. 7.25

(2) Slowly and smoothly raise the upper body (along with the arms) and the legs off the ground by about six inches.

(3) Hold this position for a count of five.

(4) Then, slowly lower your body to the ground.

(5) Repeat this exercise five times.

Notes : (1) Do not pursue the exercise too vigorously or jerk your body up.

(2) Do not raise the body more than recommended.

At the end of the fourth week, take the back fitness tests again. You will find, to your joy, that you have, finally, achieved the 'excellent' grade in all the tests.

Now your muscles are strong yet supple enough to hold constantly your pelvis and the lower spine in a balanced position, making your back immune to problems and injuries.

You have won the first round of your battle against backache !

---

8. MAINTENANCE OF BACK-FITNESS

If you have intelligently and religiously followed the exercise programme recommended in chapter 7, you will tremendously gain in strength and stamina. Needless to say, you will then succeed in achieving the 'excellent' grade in all 'back-fitness tests'. Now there will be a natural temptation to let up. After all, you have won the battle, isn't it? Yes, but only for the time-being.

Remember 'That which is used develops; that which is not, wastes away'. In other words, 'use it or lose it'. This wise statement has been confirmed again and again by medical researchers. The marvellous human machine is different from other machines in that it improves the more you put it to use – within reasonable limits, of course. Maintaining dynamic back-fitness and general fitness can be a difficult task in an affluent and mechanized society with numerous so called 'convenience gadgets' readily at hand. We must counter the undesirable effects of our sedentary living with a daily session of exercises that will provide and replace what our bodies are missing. Otherwise, our muscles weaken and our body succumbs to the relentless ageing process at an accelerated rate.

What is the result when people fail to exercise and build up or maintain stamina ? They gradually fall a prey to stress and lapse into a state of negative health balance. They succumb to avoidable sickness and premature ageing manifested by overweight, high blood pressure, high neuromuscular tension, fast pulse rate, low adrenocortical reserve, low breathing capacity, low muscle-strength and flexibility, low heart strength and low emotional stability. They become ready victims to not only low back pain but also to other disorders like ulcers, colitis, tension headaches, nervous disorders, obesity, impotence and heart disease. The only way to fend off the sinister but subtle influence of the sedentary life is to become and remain active by doing purposeful physical exercise on a regular basis.

The back maintenance programme that follows is designed to keep your back and body fit. We define fitness as 'readiness for action'. Think about the people you know who are in good physical shape. What qualities do they possess that an unfit person does not have ? Stamina springs first to our mind — the ability to work and play for long periods without fatigue. Coupled with stamina, you will usually find slimness. The reason these two qualities go hand in hand is fairly obvious. People who work or play for long periods of time because of good endurance burn off a lot of calories. After such hard workouts, they can eat large meals and yet not gain even an ounce.

The next two qualities that come to mind when discussing fitness are strength and flexibility. Muscles that are not regularly used lose both these capabilities. True fitness, therefore, consists of four qualities :

stamina and slimness balanced with strength and flexibility. All these qualities can be easily imbibed if you resolve to perform regularly the maintenance exercises described here. They are safe, simple and efficient and will not consume more than a few minutes each day.

(1) Lateral Stretch : This exercise stretches and strengthens the lateral muscles i.e., the muscles at the sides of the trunk.

Starting Position : Stand keeping a distance of about two feet between the two feet. Keep the arms by the sides of the body.

Procedure : (1) Raise the right arm above your head and slowly bend your trunk towards the left. The left palm should slide down the side of your thigh towards the knee.

(2) After bending the trunk as much as possible, return to the original position, with the arms at the side.

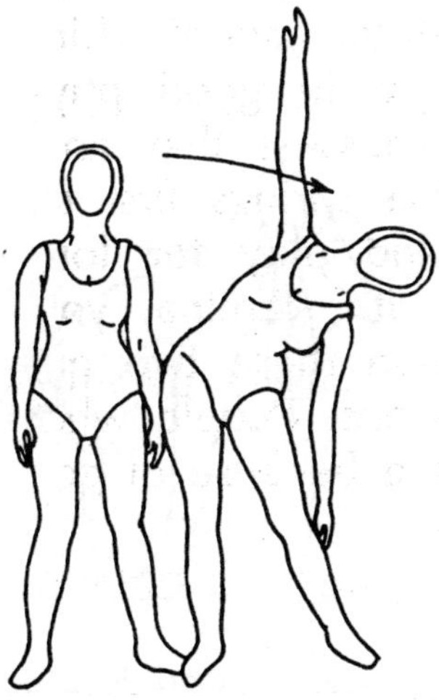

side-bending exercise for the spine

Fig. 8.1

(3) Now reverse the movements raising the left arm above the head, bending the trunk towards the right and sliding the right palm down the side of the thigh towards the knee. Return to the original position.

(4) Repeat five times.

Note : The entire motion should be slow, non-jerky and smooth; otherwise, the lateral muscles may get stained.

(2) Back Stretch : This exercise stretches the back muscles, the hip extensors and the hamstring muscles. It also strengthens the back muscles.

Starting Position : Stand keeping a distance of about two feet between the two feet. Keep your arms raised above your head.

Procedure : (1) Slowly bend your arms and the body forward and downward, in an arc.

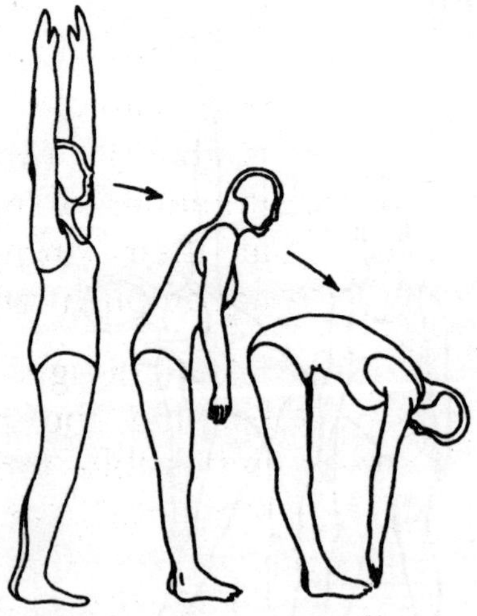

exercising the thoracic and lumbar areas of the spine

Fig. 8.2

(2) Smoothly and without putting undue strain on the back, stoop as much as possible.

(3) Slowly return to the original position.

(4) Repeat five times.

Note : Do not try to reach the ground with a forceful jerk; that may result into back stain.

(3) Quadriceps Stretch : Quadriceps are muscles at the front of the thighs. Strong quadriceps protect the back when you lift a heavy object. This exercise stretches and strengthens the quadriceps.

Starting Position : Stand with your back and buttocks against the wall. Keep your feet about two feet away from the wall.

Procedure : (1) Keeping the back in contact with the wall, slowly bend your legs at the knees. Your back will slide downward along the wall. Bend the knees till your thighs are perpendicular to the wall. In this position, your body seems to be resting on an imaginary chair.

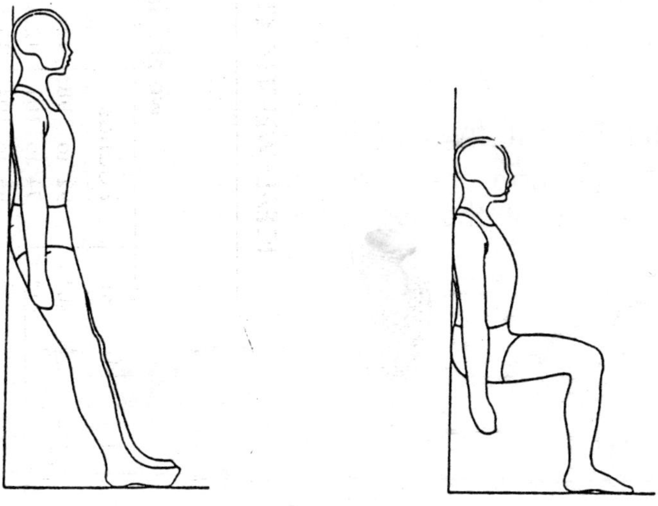

Fig. 8.3

(2) Hold this position for a minute or two.

(3) Return to the original (i.e., standing) position.

(4) Repeat the movement two to three times.

Note : The movement should be smooth and nonjerky, especially while returning (from sitting) to the standing position.

(4) Racer Stretch : This exercise stretches the hip flexors and the calf muscles, both of which are important postural muscles. When shortened (as is usually the case), they prevent the pelvis from reaching a balanced position.

Starting Position : Assume the racer's starting position, with the left leg below the chest and the right leg extended backward as far as possible.

Procedure : (1) Slowly allow the body to move down towards the ground.

(2) All the time, keep the back straight and the left foot firmly planted on the ground.

(3) Feel the muscles of the right hip and both calves stretch.

(4) Hold for five counts.

(5) Return to the original, high position.

(6) Repeat five times.

(7) Perform the exercise five times more, with the positions of the legs reversed.

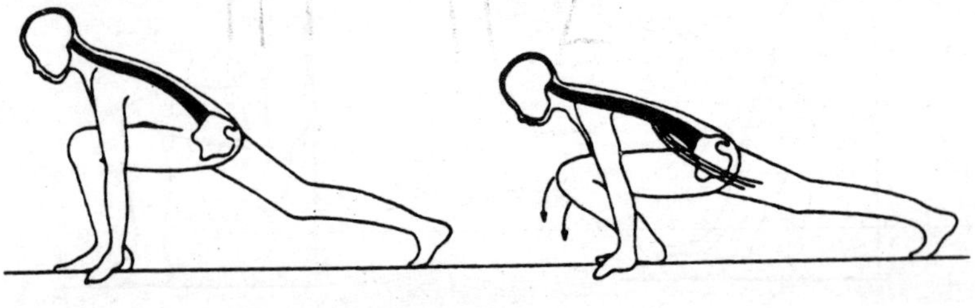

Fig. 8.4

Notes : (1) Keep the back straight throughout the exercise. Place the weight of your trunk on your fore-foot.

(2) Exhale at the last part of stretching to get maximum benefits.

(5) Mad Cat : This exercise improves mobility of the spine and relieves stiffness or tension in the lower back.

Starting Position : Kneel on the ground with hands planted on the ground.

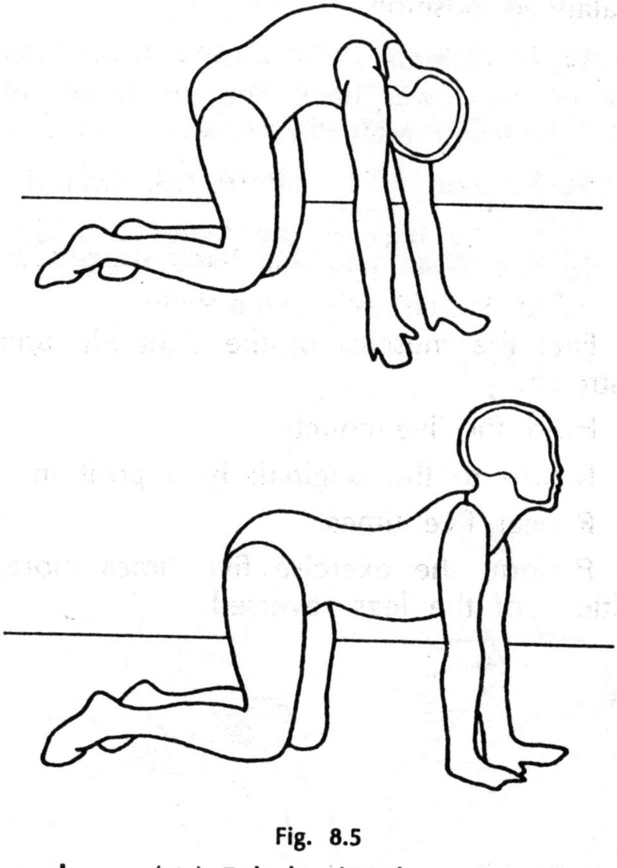

Fig. 8.5

Procedure : (1) Exhale deeply and pull down your back (from the straight position) to a concave position.

Your back should form an arc with the head and buttocks pointing upwards and the mid-back pointing downwards.

(2) Next, inhale deeply and reverse the arch of the back so that your chin and the tail-bone point downwards and the mid-back points upwards.

(3) Return to the original position.

(4) Repeat five times.

Note : If this exercise produces discomfort, ease off i.e., do not stretch the back fully. Gradually work up to a full stretch.

(6) Groin Stretch : This exercise improves the flexibility of the lower back and stretches the groin (perineum) and hip adductor muscles.

Starting Position : (1) Sit on the ground.

(2) Bend the legs at the knees and bring the soles of the two feet in contact. The heels should lie as close to the groin as possible.

(3) Rest your elbows on your knees.

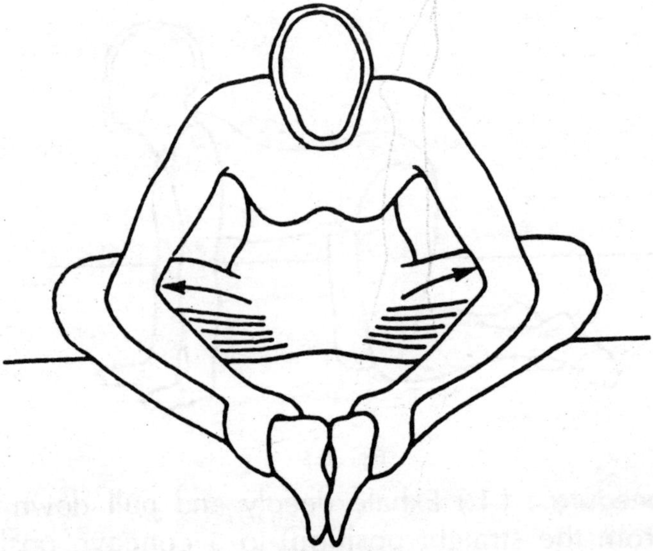

Fig. 8.6

Procedure : (1) In a smooth and non-jerky effort, push the knees downwards (towards the floor) with the elbows. At the same time, pull the heels towards the groin and stoop slightly forward.

(2) Hold for five counts and then relax.

(3) Repeat five times.

Note : The exercise is somewhat difficult. Do not use excessive force or a jerk to stretch the inner thigh muscles.

(7) Maximum leg lift in side-lying position : This exercise strengthens the muscles at the side of the trunk and the right arm to balance your body.

Fig. 8.7

Procedure : (1) Balance the pelvis.

(2) Raise both legs about six inches off the ground.

(3) Hold this position.

(4) Slowly raise the upper (right) leg as far towards the ceiling as possible.

(5) Slowly return the upper leg to the lower one.

(6) Repeat five times.

(7) Repeat the entire procedure lying on your right side.

Note : Maintain correct pelvic tilt (i.e., balance) throughout the exercise. That will ensure that your body lies in a straight line when you move your legs.

(8) Hamstrings Stretch : This exercise stretches the hamstrings muscles which lie at the back of the thigh. These are key postural muscles.

Starting Position : Lie down on the ground with knees bent at about 45 degrees and feet planted on the ground. Keep the arms on the ground by the sides of the body.

Procedure : (1) Draw your left knee towards your chest, keeping the right foot planted on the ground.

(2) Extend (straighten) this leg upwards with the toes pointing towards the ceiling.

(3) Keeping the leg extended, bend only your foot towards your head.

(4) Slowly take the leg down to the ground keeping it straight.

(5) Finally, bring it back to the starting (knee-bent) position.

(6) Now perform the movements with the right leg, keeping the left foot planted on the ground.

(7) Repeat five times with each leg.

Fig. 8.8

Note : During the entire movement, maintain the pelvis in a balanced position.

(9) Cycling movements in lying position : This exercise strengthens the abdominal and most of the leg muscles. It also stretches and relaxes the muscles of the middle and lower back.

Starting Position : Lie down on the ground with knees bent at about 45 degrees and feet planted on the ground.

Procedure : (1) Draw the right knee towards the chest.

(2) At the same time, move the left leg away from the body so that it straightens somewhat. Note that the lower surface of the thigh and the calf should not come in contact with the ground.

(3) Next reverse the roles of the legs.

(4) Continue for a minute or two.

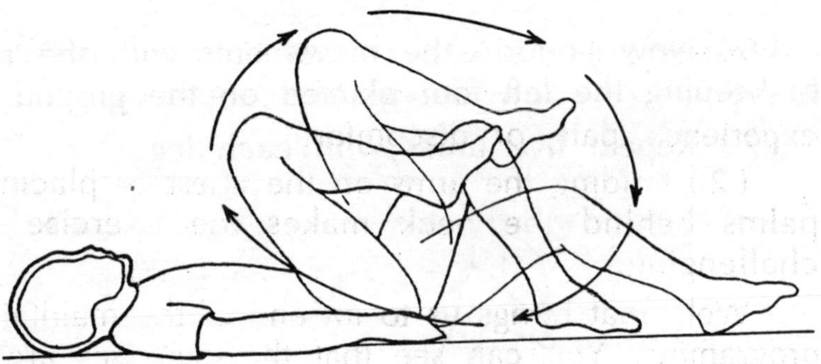

Fig. 8.9

Note : The movement resembles cycling. It should be smooth and slow.

(10) bent leg sit-up : This exercise strengthens the abdominal muscles and improves the flexibility of the lower back.

Starting Position : (1) Lie down on the ground with the knees bent at about 45 degrees and feet planted on the ground.

(2) Extend your arms in front of your body (not over your head).

Procedure : (1) Assume the pelvic balance.

(2) Keeping your feet firmly planted on the ground, rise slowly to a sitting position. Refrain from jerking up the body.

(3) Slowly and carefully lower your body back to the ground curling fully back into the balanced pelvis position, with the chin held against the chest.

(4) Relax and repeat five times.

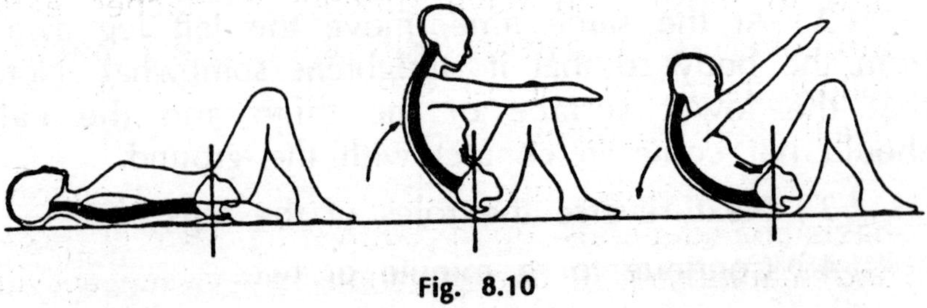

Fig. 8.10

Notes : (1) If you do not hold the pelvis in a balanced position during the exercise, you may experience pain or discomfort.

(2) Folding the arms on the chest or placing the palms behind the neck makes the exercise more challenging.

Well, that brings us to an end of the maintenance programme. You can see that the exercises are easy and don't consume much time. They can be used to warm up the muscles and the body before engaging in any sport. They are also excellent tension relievers after a hard day over a hot desk.

Perform these exercises regularly every day. Remember that consistency is the key to fitness.

---

9. PREVENTION OF BACKACHE

It is said that 'Prevention is better than cure'. We would like to add that it is cheaper, too. Preventing diseases like diabetes, cancer or heart disease entails drastic steps like altering life-style or giving up certain foods and other things which contribute to make the life more pleasurable. Preventing back problems, on the other hand, is much simpler. Tips for prevention that have been given here will prove useful not only to persons who have had no back problems so far but also to those who have suffered backaches earlier. Moreover, if a person with an existing backache follow these tips, he or she will be able to regain health and happiness faster.

At the outset, we will state that prevention of backache depends upon cultivating correct posture and maintaining it during various day-to-day activities.

And let us remind you that maintenance of good posture is a function of strong and supple muscles of the back and the abdomen. These qualities of the muscles can be attained or maintained by regularly performing the exercises recommended in chapters 7 and 8.

People's foggy and fallacious notions about good posture once used to surprise and irritate us. It took long for us to realize that posture does not figure high on most people's list of priorities. They are far more interested in reducing weight, building muscles, bleaching the face or trimming eye-brows. Such gross ignorance about benefits of good posture and hazards of an incorrect one can also be attributed to the fact that neither teaching institutions nor health institutions educate people about posture and its relation with backache.

How much do you think you know about good posture ? Let us put you to the test. If asked to stand up straight, what would you do ? Well, if you are like the majority of our patients, you will adopt a 'military' stance, with shoulders pulled back and the chest thrust forward, creating a steep hollow in the lower back and making the buttocks to bulge out. We just can't understand where such mistaken belief about good posture sprang from. May be your P.T. or N.C.C. teacher planted such ideas in your mind. Please understand that such an 'at-attention' way of standing is not a good posture at all. In fact, it is an unnatural way to hold the body and will cause fatigue and pain if maintained for long periods of time.

Let us, then, examine and understand what good posture is. A person's posture can be considered good when (1) the shoulders are held slightly back (but still in line with the chest), (2) the chin is tucked in and (3) the hollow at the lower back is somewhat flattened by a contraction of the abdominal muscles.

To evaluate your own posture, stand sideways in front of a full-length mirror with a minimum of clothes. View your body dispassionately.

Imagine a plumb line hanging from the ceiling; it represents a line of force through your body's centre of gravity. The line should fall behind the ear, the nape of the neck, the base of the back behind the hip, in front of the knee and down through the centre of your ankle (see Fig. 9.1)

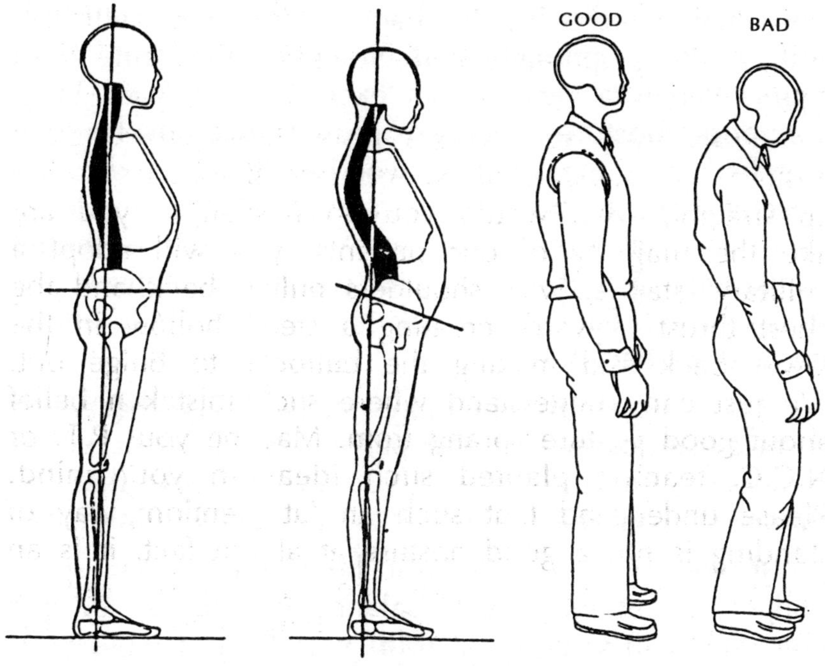

Fig. 9.1

If your body falls primarily behind or in front of the line, you have a poor posture. Do you have rounded shoulders ? Does your upper back protrude backward ? Do you have an excessive hollow in the lower back ? Does your belly protrude forward ? Do your buttocks stick out ? Then you have poor posture.

We grant that these facts may disappoint or dismay you. But take comfort in the fact that in a few weeks' time, you are going to look and feel much better. You will look as good from the sides as you do from the front.

Good posture hinges on the pelvic tilt. When the pelvis is held in a balanced position (see chapters 2 and 7 again), the back automatically curves normally and all parts of the body attain a state of balance. In this state, all the muscles of the body, and especially those associated with the back, are at their efficient best, working optimally and protecting the spine from injury. When a person has excessively curved back (i.e., poor posture), certain groups of muscles are stretched past the optimal working length and other muscles have to take an extra work. For example, if the abdominal muscles are weak, the pelvis is shifted forward causing the back and psoas (hip) muscles to be over-used. Such over-work produces chronic fatigue leading to backache.

At the cost of repetition, we will say that good posture centres around the pelvic tilt. Put your pelvis in a balanced position and you will observe that the curves in your back reduce to a healthy minimum.

If you want to see just how much your spine straightens out when you balance the pelvis, try this stint. Stand in your usual (old) posture and have your friend mark your height on the wall with a pencil. Now tilt the pelvis to a balanced position. Press the small of your back as flat as you can against the wall, pull in your stomach, take your shoulders slightly back and hold your head straight up. You will discover that you have grown an inch, perhaps two.

We showed this trick to one of our patients. He was really impressed. We recommended that he maintain the pelvic balance and the correct posture in his day-to-day activities. He came back after two days complaining that it was not easy for him to maintain correct posture for any reasonable length of time. "I am so used to the wrong way that the right way feels wrong," he said.

We understood exactly what he meant. If you have been holding your body incorrectly for years, it has become second nature to you – it feels right. That is because posture is a habit. But remember you were not born with a bad posture. You developed it, as you grew, due to various influences.

Habits can be unlearned or changed – for the better. If you consciously practise good posture for some days, it will become automatic. It will then become a part of your life, something you no longer need to remain conscious or aware of.

However, understand one thing clearly : Unless you strengthen weak muscles and stretch short muscles, you won't be able to attain pelvic balance and correct posture in spite of all your efforts.

Once you have accomplished good posture, you will not only be able to ward off backaches but also look younger, more graceful and more elegant. Moreover, you will feel much less tired at the end of the day because your muscles are working with good co-ordination and peak efficiency.

Although the basic cause of back trouble is, of course, weak back muscles, it is possible to get along without problems as long as those weak muscles are not called upon to perform beyond their capacity. If, however, they are suddenly required to take on a heavy job (e.g., lifting) or awkwardly stretched, they will give in, producing discomfort and pain. Even when back muscles are in good shape, lifting or doing something awkwardly or incorrectly can hurt the back because stresses and loads are placed upon the wrong part of the spine.

"How am I to know if I am doing the various common activities correctly or not ?", you are bound to ask. Your question is quite correct. Indeed, the knowledge about the method of correctly performing common tasks will go a long way to avoiding sudden back strain and, thereby, preventing a back problem.

Various "authorities" and experts have formulated and presented some rules which, if followed while performing tasks involving back muscles, minimize chances of injury. On close scrutiny, these rules can be boiled down to just one key factor : adopt and maintain the balanced pelvic tilt (position) throughout a task.

Patients, however, ask for specific tips. With a view to satisfying them we shall describe here the do's and don't's to be followed while performing some common tasks. Please understand once again, however, that these precautions are complementary and not a substitute to specific exercise programme for strengthening the muscles associated with the back.

(1) Lifting : Most back injuries are blamed on lifting things the wrong way. However, as we saw in chapter 3, awkward lifting is only a minor culprit, the major one being weak back muscles that prove unequal to the task. In any case, correct lifting techniques should be learned and put into practice.

Rules for safe lifting, formulated by back-care and occupational medicine experts, stress that a person should :

* size up the load before attempting the lift,
* balance with feet wide apart,
* bend the knees,
* keep the back straight,
* grip the object firmly,
* hold the load close to the body and
* avoid twisting the body.

Before we elaborate on these rules, we will say that our spine, as it is, has a lot of burden to carry. If you can help it, don't lift or carry a weight exceeding ten kilograms. Well, that may not sound practicable to you. We are all obliged to lift and carry weights many times during the day.

Fig. 9.2

Most people automatically lift the wrong way — they bend their back while lifting, keeping the knees and the arms straight. That subjects the spine to a heavy stress. The correct lifting technique entails (a) bending the knees and the hips, keeping the back straight, (b) lifting with the knees (which are much more capable of coping with a load) and not with the back and (c) keeping the elbows bent so that the weight remains close to the body. It is not generally known or realized that your arms are much stronger if they are close to your body. Interestingly, this is one of the basic principles of judo – in which a 'judoka' will rarely try to lift his opponent off the ground unless he has first pulled him close to himself. This same principle should be used to lift any weight.

There come times when you are forced to lift awkwardly, e.g., unloading something from the dickey of a car, lifting a baby out of a crib, etc. At such times, ensure that no twisting or movement of the spine takes place. This is easy if you stabilize your trunk in a balanced pelvis position.

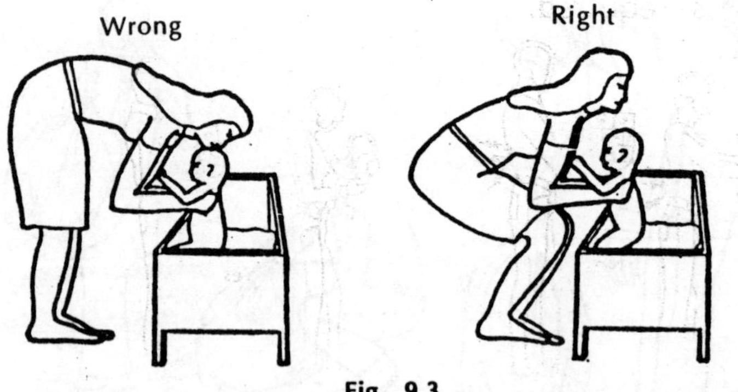

Fig. 9.3

On occasions, you have to lift an object that is lying at a height (e.g., a housewife trying to lift a container lying on a high kitchen-shelf). You will notice that when you are lifting objects above your head, your spine begins to arch. That is a signal to get a stool or a ladder so that the lifting can be accomplished in the classical fashion – with arms bent.

Fig. 9.4

After lifting the object, you may have to carry it through some distance. Keep the object close to the body. That minimises the strain on the back muscles. Try holding a chair with your arms stretched out. Next hold it close to your body and see how much less effort is required.

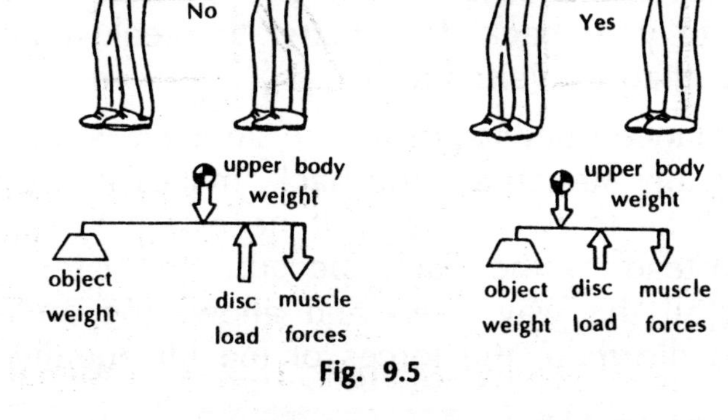

Fig. 9.5

Hold the object you are carrying, at the belly or navel level. Certainly avoid carrying the object above your shoulders or on the head because that arches the spine.

During a journey or after shopping, carry almost equal loads in the two hands. That balances the body and the spine.

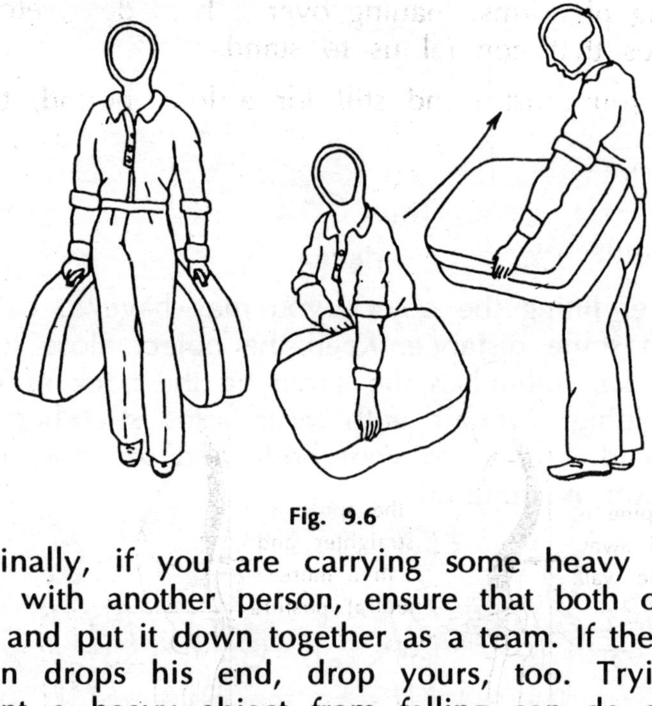

Fig. 9.6

Finally, if you are carrying some heavy object along with another person, ensure that both of you lift it and put it down together as a team. If the other person drops his end, drop yours, too. Trying to prevent a heavy object from falling can do serious damage to your back. It is better to break a piece of furniture than a vertebra.

A balanced pelvis position, if adopted while lifting, automatically straightens the back, makes it impossible for the spine to twist, makes it necessary to bend the knees instead of the back (because the later cannot be bent all the way over) and allows the abdominal cavity to distribute the forces of the lift equally in all directions (the hydraulic sac principle), thereby saving the spine from excessive stress. In other words, if the back is stabilized in the balanced pelvic position, safe lifting technique becomes automatic. You don't have to think consciously about its application.

(2) Standing : Prolonged standing in a fixed position may cause discomfort in the back. Waiting for a public vehicle, ironing, washing up, cooking on standing platforms, leaning over a high desk, etc. are activities that compel us to stand.

If you must stand still for a long period, try to rest one foot higher than the other; that brings the pelvis into a balanced position, flattening the hollow of the back. This reduces the strain on the back muscles.

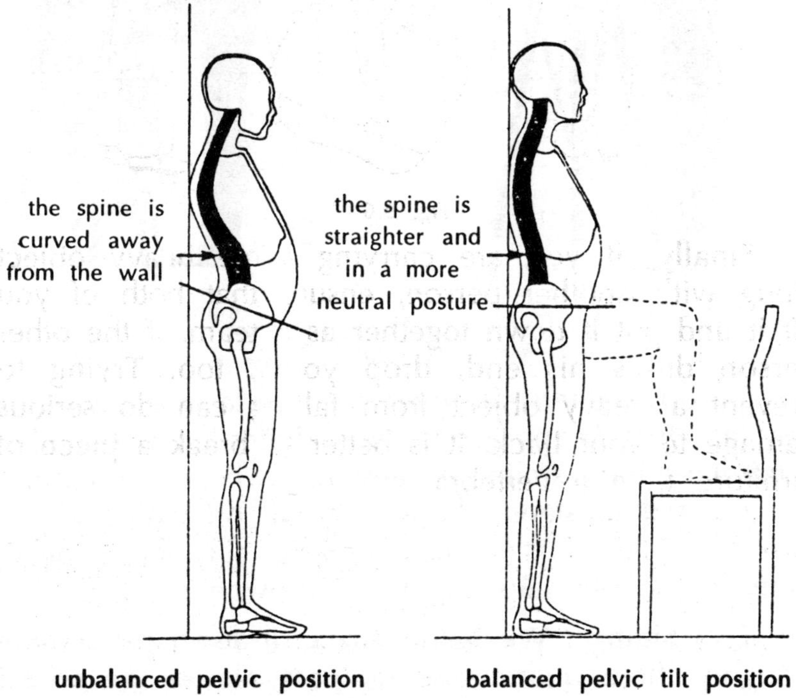

Fig. 9.7

For example, if you are working on a ladder, put one foot on a rung higher than the other. If you are waiting at a railway station or an airport, rest one foot on your suitcase. If you have no suitcase or other luggage, bend one knee and keep the other straight. In fact, people instictively adopt such posture while waiting. While ironing, or cooking, put one foot on a small stool.

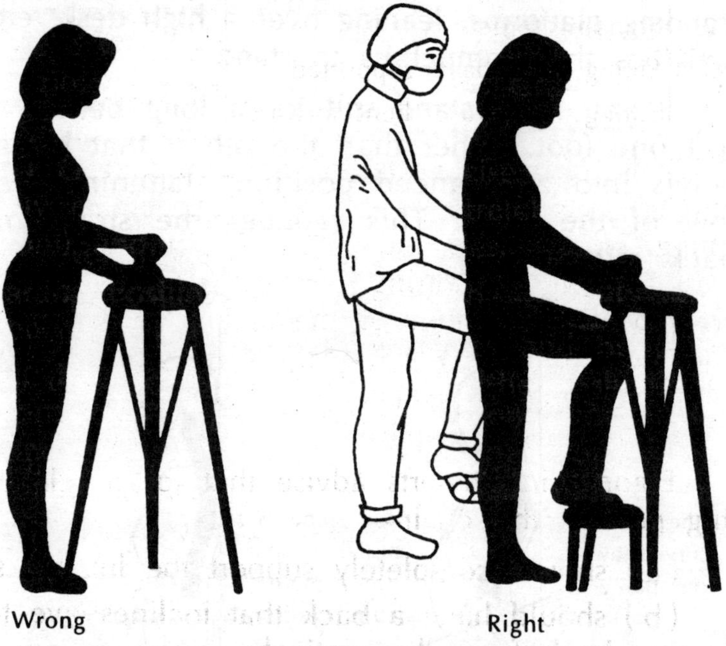

Fig. 9.8

Tavern-keepers all over the world are aware of the fact that keeping one foot higher than the other minimizes back-strain. At any bar where the patrons are obliged to stand, there is a rail on which a foot can be rested. Customers, therefore, stay for a longer time in the bar fattening the bar-owner's purse !

(3) Sitting : We belong to a sit-down generation. Roughly three quarters of us pass almost the whole day in sitting position – at work and at our homes.

At the beginning of this century, the idea gradually emerged that the efficiency of the workers might improve if they are provided with seats. It was discovered only recently that sitting postures exert more pressure on the discs of the spine than the standing posture as shown below :

No.	Posture	Pressure on the disc
1	Lying flat on the back	24
2	Standing erect	100
3	Sitting with back supported	140
4	Sitting with trunk bent forward	190

It is for this reason that some experts are of the opinion that man's spine was not really designed for sitting. However, in today's world, one can't think of working without sitting. Hence, we should pay a great deal of attention to the factors of 'where to sit' and 'how to sit'. That branch of science which deals with moulding the shape of the furniture (for example, chairs) to suit our spines is termed 'ergonomics'.

Ergonomics experts advise that for a relaxed sitting posture the chair—

(a) should completely support the lumbar spine,

(b) should have a back that inclines five to ten degrees back from the vertical,

(c) should have a firm seat whose height is such as allows the feet to be planted on the floor, with knees remaining at a slightly higher level than the hips (i.e., you should be able to place your palm between the seat and the back of your lower thigh),

(d) should not have a seat excessively long (deep), not allowing your lumbar spine to come in contact with the back rest and

(e) should preferably have arm—rests at the sides.

For good back support, the back of the chair should have a S-curve, resembling that of the spine. In practice, it may be difficult to find a chair which satisfactorily serves this purpose because the bends of the 'S' may be at different levels in different people. But you can buy a lumbar support cushion that fits neatly into the hollow of your lower spine and certainly increases your comfort. There are chairs that have adjustable back supports; these are helpful.

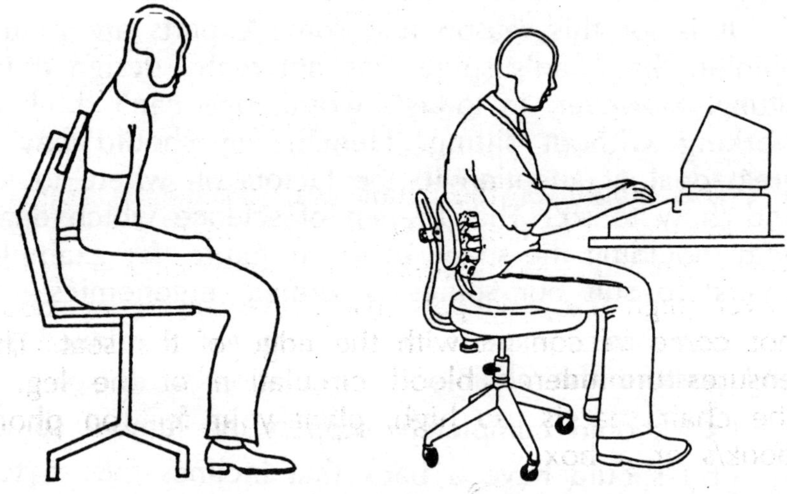

Wrong Right

Fig. 9.9

A chair that is permanently inclined back by about ten degrees or that can be tilted backward when desired takes weight off the spine and relaxes the back muscles.

The seat of the chair should be only lightly padded, if at all. A soft seat allows the body to sink down, causing undesirable flexure (swaying or hollowing) of the lumbar spine.

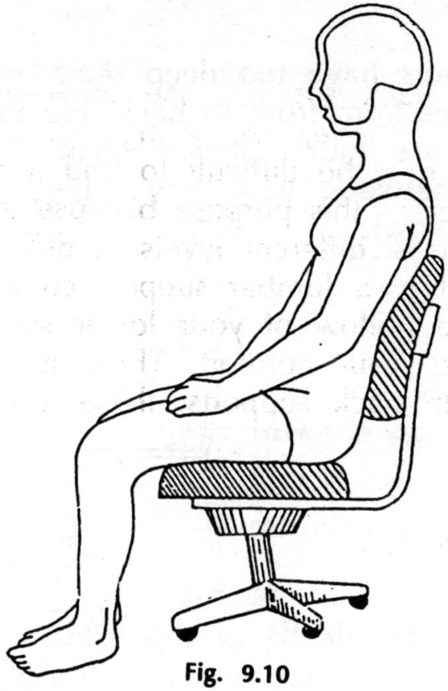

Fig. 9.10

The height of the chair seat should be such as would allow the feet to be planted on the floor, with knees bent at 90 degrees. The undersurface of the lower thigh (i.e., the part just above the knee) should not come in contact with the edge of the seat. This ensures unhindered blood circulation of the leg. If the chair seat is too high, plant your feet on phone book/s or a box.

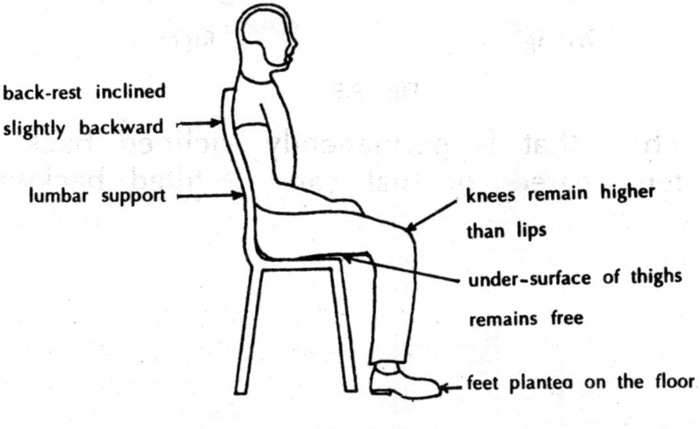

Fig. 9.11

Many chairs have too deep seats, measuring almost 20 inches from front to back. Human thighs, on an average, are much shorter than this, resulting into a gap between your lower back and chair's back (see below).

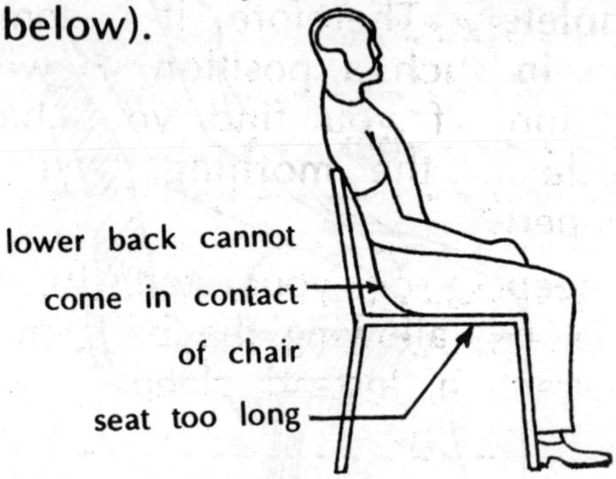

Fig. 9.12

Actually, the depth of the chair's seat should be around 15–16 inches and certainly not more than 17 inches.

With that, we have come to an end of the description of a good chair – the one which will prove kind to the back. You should check out if the chairs you use at home and at work satisfy these conditions. After all, you are going to spend more than half your life sitting down. However, even a good chair will do little good to a person who does not sit properly. The diagrams given below are self-explanatory.

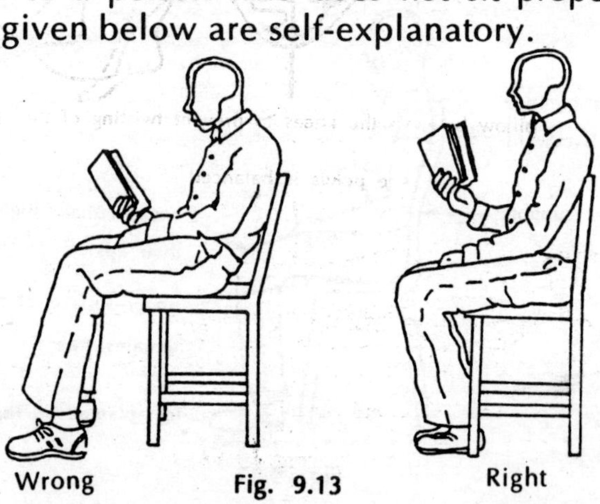

Fig. 9.13

(4) Sleeping : This subheading may come as a surprise. Is good posture important even when one is sleeping ? The answer comes in an affirmative. It is only when you lie down, does the back get a chance to rest completely. Therefore, it becomes necessary to lie down in such a position as would promote total relaxation. If you find your back stiff and uncomfortable in the morning, you may not be sleeping properly.

Avoid sleeping on your stomach; it arches the lumbar spine, not allowing the back muscles to give up their contraction. Instead, sleep on your side, with the knees and the hips bent comfortably. If you like to lie down on your back, support your knees over one or more pillows so that the pelvis is put in a balanced position.

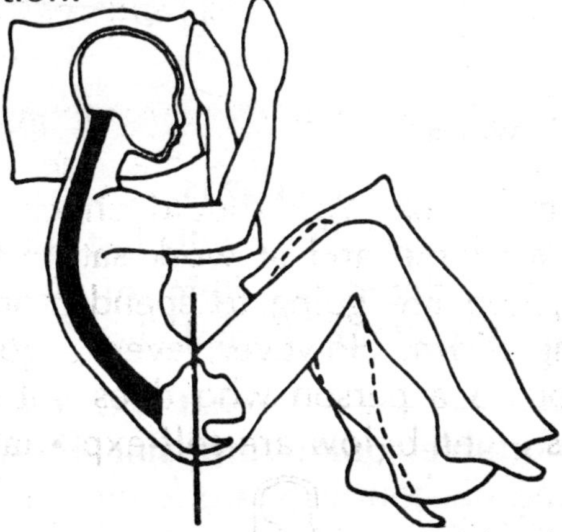

pillow between the knees to prevent twisting of the spine

the pelvis is balanced

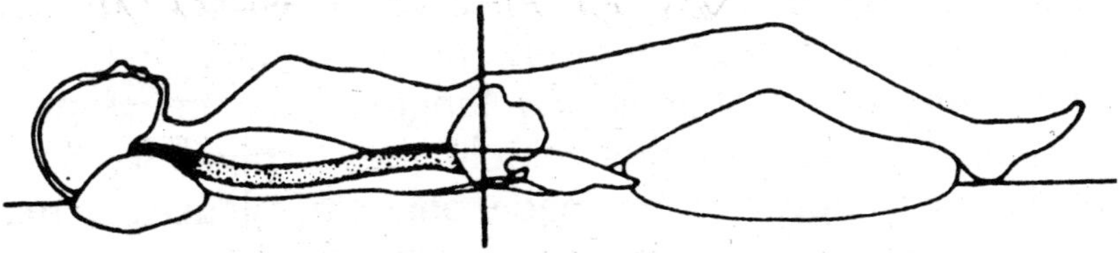

knees bent and comfortable supported by a pillow

Fig. 9.14

Do not use so soft a matress as would allow the body to sag. That is the reason why you should never sleep on a sofa. Do not use too thick a pillow under your head. If, unfortunately, your mattress is too soft, place a plywood bedboard under it.

Do not lay your little one in a cloth cradle which makes its spine arch unnaturally. Instead, use a flat-floored, wooden or metal cradle.

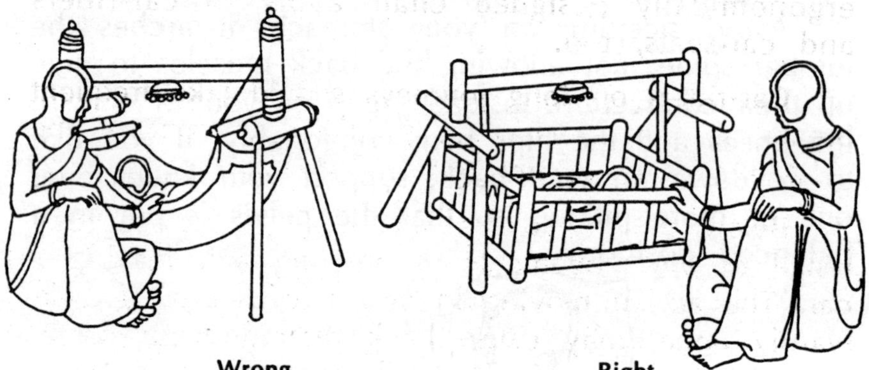

Fig. 9.15

(5) Car : In big cities with fast life, a car can no longer be considered an item of luxury. Indeed, it has become a part of normal life.

We can't help stating that the seats of most cars are uncomfortable, quite surprising if we consider the fact that long car-journeys are known to cause stiffness and back-discomfort. A seat suitable for a long-legged man may be totally unsuitable for a short-legged lady. Though the owner or driver may get his car-seat adjusted to suit himself, his passengers who are of varying sizes, shapes and lengths have to adapt as best as they can to the vehicle they travel in. Some back seats appear to be made only for midgets; a man who is slightly over-size faces great difficulty getting in and has to travel with his head and back bent and knees up, pressing against the back of the front seat. Although the foetus, in its mother's womb, can tolerate such position for several months, any adult male or female is likely to experience discomfort soon. The back seat of many cars is actually the backache seat !

Without elaborating any further, we shall state that the qualities of good sitting posture and an ergonomically designed chair apply to car-riders and car-seats, too.

Car-riders on long journeys should take frequent breaks, during which they should come out of the vehicle and flex their limbs.

Before moving to the next topic, a passing reference to the movements of entering and leaving a car. The act of moving in or out of a car, if awkwardly done, may cause back discomfort or sometimes even acute pain. A good procedure is to get in and out of the car much as you would get in and out of your bed. When entering a car, first sit sideways on the edge of the seat with your feet outside on the ground. Then lean back so that your head clears the doorway and enters the car. Finally, gently swing your legs inside. To get out, reverse the order of movements : First swing your feet sideways and out on to the ground, then lean forward enough to clear the doorway and finally stand up.

(6) Household chores : All household chores can be accomplished easily and safely if the housewife remembers to hold her pelvis in a balanced position. In this position, it is impossible to bend or twist the spine sufficiently to strain the back muscles.

Here is an example that demonstrates how the pelvic tilt protects the back :

(a) Stand with your feet about a foot apart.

(b) Tighten your abdominal muscles and assume the balanced pelvic position.

(c) Twist from your waist while holding the pelvic balance.

You will notice that you can't bend too much forward or sideways if you hold your pelvis in the balanced state.

It is easy to forget the 'don't twist while you lift' rule. But if you maintain the pelvis in a balanced position, your back will 'remember' for you. The muscles will not allow the spine to be used in a vulnerable position.

However, with a view to satisfying specific requests, we have shown below correct and incorrect ways of performing common house-hold tasks :

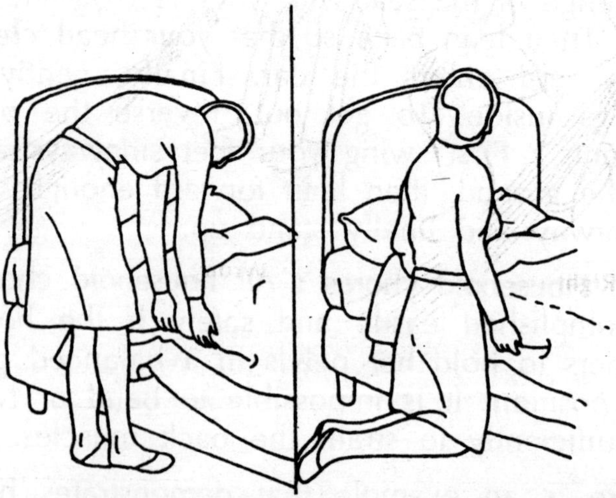

Wrong Right

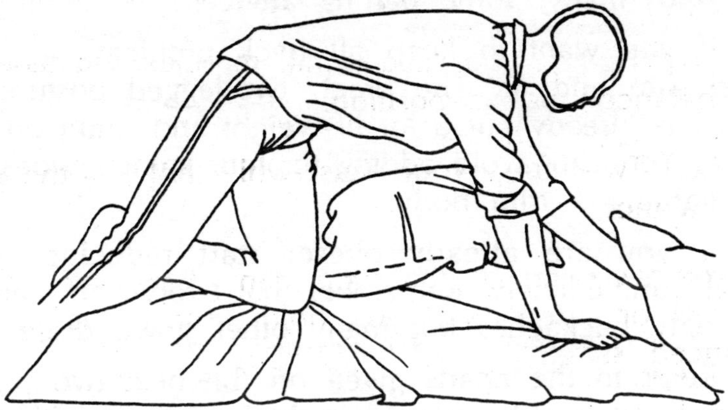

Right

Fig. 9.16

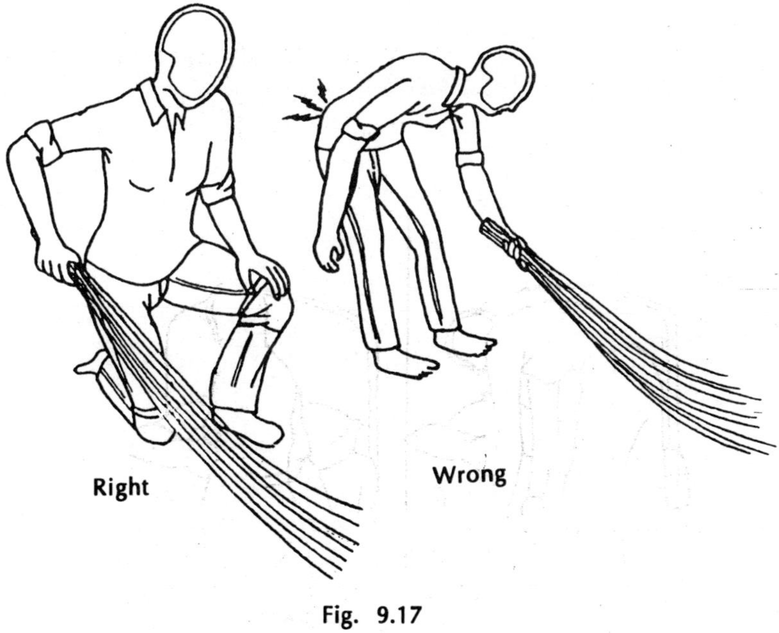

Fig. 9.17

And finally, some parting advice :

If you want to keep all back problems at bay, keep slim and fit. The erect, two-legged posture of man has already put a lot of weight and strain on his spine. You can avoid adding to your spine's woes by maintaining a trim body.

If you are already obese, start reducing your weight immediately. Remember that overweight causes not only backaches but many other grave diseases.

Refer to the charts given on the next two pages to find out whether your weight is correct with respect to your height and build or excessive.

---

* Details about scientific ways of reducing weight have been given in the book 'From Fat to Fit' by the present authors.

IDEAL WEIGHT CHART FOR MEN AGED 25 AND ABOVE

Height		Small frame weight in		Medium frame weight in		Large frame weight in	
Cm	Ft.-inch	Pounds	Kg	Pounds	Kg	Pounds	Kg
158	5′ 2"	111 to 120	50.5 to 54.5	118 to 129	53.5 to 58.5	126 to 141	57 to 64
160	3"	115 to 123	52 to 56	121 to 133	55 to 61	129 to 144	58.5 to 65
163	4"	118 to 126	53.5 to 57	124 to 136	56 to 62	132 to 148	60 to 67
165	5"	121 to 129	55 to 58.5	127 to 139	57.5 to 63	135 to 152	61 to 69
168	6"	124 to 133	56 to 60	130 to 143	58.5 to 65	138 to 156	62.5 to 71
170	7"	128 to 137	58 to 62	134 to 147	60 to 66.5	142 to 161	64.5 to 73
173	8"	132 to 141	60 to 64	138 to 152	62.5 to 69	147 to 166	66.5 to 75
175	9"	136 to 145	62 to 66	142 to 156	64.5 to 71	151 to 169	68.5 to 77
178	10"	140 to 150	63.5 to 68	146 to 160	66 to 72.5	155 to 174	70 to 79
180	11"	144 to 154	65 to 70	150 to 165	68 to 75	159 to 179	72 to 81
183	6′ 0"	148 to 158	67 to 71.5	154 to 170	70 to 77	164 to 184	74 to 83.5
185	1"	152 to 162	69 to 73.5	157 to 175	71.5 to 79	168 to 189	76 to 85.5
188	2"	156 to 167	71 to 76	162 to 180	73.5 to 81.5	173 to 194	78.5 to 88
190	3"	160 to 171	72.5 to 77.5	167 to 185	76 to 84	178 to 199	80.5 to 90.5
193	4"	164 to 175	74 to 79	172 to 190	78 to 86	182 to 204	82.5 to 92.5

IDEAL WEIGHT CHART FOR WOMEN AGED 25 AND ABOVE

Height		Small frame weight in		Medium frame weight in		Large frame weight in	
Cm	Ft.-inch	Pounds	Kg	Pounds	Kg	Pounds	Kg
147	4′ 10"	92 to 98	42 to 44.5	96 to 107	43.5 to 48.5	104 to 119	47 to 54
150	11"	94 to 101	42.5 to 46	98 to 110	44.5 to 50	106 to 122	48 to 55
152	5′ 0"	96 to 104	43.5 to 47	101 to 113	46 to 51	109 to 125	49.5 to 56.5
155	1"	99 to 107	45 to 48.5	104 to 116	47 to 52.5	112 to 128	51 to 58
158	2"	102 to 110	46.5 to 50	107 to 119	48.5 to 54	115 to 131	52 to 59.5
160	3"	105 to 113	47.5 to 51	110 to 122	50 to 55	118 to 134	53.5 to 61
163	4"	108 to 116	49 to 52.5	113 to 126	51 to 57	121 to 138	55 to 62
165	5"	111 to 119	50.5 to 54	116 to 130	52.5 to 58.5	125 to 142	57 to 64.5
168	6"	114 to 123	52 to 56	120 to 135	54.5 to 61	129 to 146	58.5 to 66
170	7"	118 to 127	53.5 to 57.5	124 to 139	56 to 63	133 to 150	60 to 68
173	8"	122 to 131	55 to 59.5	128 to 143	58 to 65	137 to 154	62 to 70
175	9"	126 to 135	57 to 61	132 to 147	60 to 66.5	141 to 158	64 to 71.5
178	10"	130 to 140	58.5 to 63.5	136 to 151	62 to 68.5	145 to 163	66 to 74
180	11"	134 to 144	61 to 65	140 to 155	63.5 to 70	149 to 168	67.5 to 76
183	6′ 0"	139 to 148	63 to 67	144 to 159	65 to 72	153 to 173	69.5 to 78.5

Ladies should abandon high-heeled sandals and shoes. Such footwear transfers or displaces the weight of the body forwards, makes the lumbar spine to arch, shortens the calf and hip-flexor muscles and increases the wear-n-tear of the spine. Remember that health is more important than fashion.

---

10. BACKACHE AND SEX

(**Important Note :** If you have backache but no sexual problems, don't read this chapter at all. We are quite serious about this. If you are not aware of any problems in this area, we don't want you to read this chapter and start thinking up problems for yourself.)

We have been dealing with backache patients for a number of years. Yet only a handful of patients have ever asked about guidelines for sex during episodes of low back pain or sciatica or have complained that their backache gets aggravated during or following a sexual intercourse. How odd, indeed ! A recent study in America at the Mayo Clinic showed that almost two-thirds of backache patients suffered from an impairment of sexual satisfaction. Sexual problems included difficulty in becoming sexually aroused and in reaching orgasm. More women were affected than men.

Obviously, many backache patients who are encountering problems with this rewarding form of human activity don't feel comfortable querrying their doctors about it. And despite all the love-making manuals that decorate book-shops, little literature is devoted to the subject of making love with a bad back. Hence, this chapter is born.

This hesitation or shyness on the part of the patient about discussing, even with the doctor, the relation between back problems and sex problems is evidenced by this letter which we received from one of our lady patients. We have abridged the letter somewhat and changed certain names and identifying details.

Dear Doctor,

I had been brought to you some time back for my back problem. In spite of the resolution that I will not hide anything from you, I could not muster enough courage to tell you about the effects my chronic backache has had on our sex relations. This letter may seem rather personal and verbose; but I have decided to disclose my story with a view to making you aware of this agonizing problem (a foreign magazine says it is quite common) so that other patients might perhaps benefit.

I used to have an antidote for being under the weather : get up, get moving, get busy. This approach set right most things. It worked for headache, colds, nausea, sore throat, menstrual cramps, flu, etc. But it has not worked for my backache.

As I lie here on the bed, I hear a crash and ensuing tears. I realize that my younger baby has fallen down. But I cannot move to soothe her, hold her and wipe away her tears. Such incidents occur quite frequently. I cannot respond to demands placed on me. My mind reacts, my body cannot. Smita no longer comes to me when she falls. She knows I cannot pick her up. In a feverish state last week, she ran to my sister-in-law Jyoti for comfort. Jyoti brought her to my bed, but she did not want to be with me.

My seven-year old son Gautam smiles on me all day. When I am on the sofa, he comes over and nuzzles me filling my face with kisses. But he does not come to me when he is thirsty, hungry or dirty. He knows who can meet his needs and who can't.

My husband expresses his mental state with occasional outbursts of temper. He is the man who relied on me for ten years; but now our roles have been reversed. He is always trying to encourage me to get well, be happy, etc. But obviously, life has become not-so-happy for him. Every now and then, there is an outburst, "I am thoroughly exhausted, I have a headache......" I guess it is quite natural for a man who has lost an exciting sex life, has given up his social life (he won't go out without me), has been under financial strain, has had his privacy taken away ...... and does not find a well-kept, will-organized home when he comes back after a long and arduous work-day. My helplessness drives me crazy, frustrated and depressed. I try to drown myself in music and books and cry myself to sleep so that I can sanely face the next day with a smile.

Sex is really a painful loss. We used to have an active, innovative and exciting sex relationship. What a great way it was to share feelings and release tensions. The most aggravating part of sexual deprivation is realizing how long it took us to reach the stage of complete freedom and passion, having lost too many years in innocence and ignorance. To be deprived of sex now is really unfair. I need and want sex; but I am afraid of hurting myself. Passive (the 'let me know when it's over') sex may be possible. But really active sex is perhaps impossible.

We have become awfully good friends. What a pitiable development it is : a helpmate surpasses a lover and loving kindness surpasses love !

I am usually reliable, emotionally stable and basically positive; but not having control over my life distresses me. I am at everyone's mercy for help and care. My independence has been taken away and self-esteem lowered.

I have not lost all hopes, though. I hope that you will have some solution for me when I visit you again next week.

With regards,

Yours sincerely,

Mrs. A. P.

This letter from a normal, intelligent and well-adjusted housewife describes the devastating side-effects of a chronic back problem. Mrs. A. P., in our opinion, was spiritually, intellectually and materially wealthy. Yet, she was only marginally able to cope with her problems.

Finally, she did conquer her bad back, largely because of her own determination. With our reassurance and guidance, she also succeeded in re-establishing satisfactory sexual relations with her husband. In conversation, Mrs. A. P. confided that previously the fear of hurting her back had been distracting her during love-making and interfered with her orgasmic response. But now she had overcome such fear.

This was a patient who had many things going for her including sexual openness, a positive attitude, a happy marriage and considerable resources both material and intellectual. How do you think a neurotic, repressed or unhappily mated person would fare ?

Sex is only one of the activities that may be cramped by chronic back pain. But since it occupies a place high up on the list, it deserves a separate chapter. Here we will analyse the sexual problems that stem directly from backache. Next we shall apply our knowledge of the pathology and biomechanics of back pain to reach a solution to the problem of deranged sex by first setting out general principles and then following up with specific recommendations for men and women with low back pain.

A sexually well adjusted person with a short-term non-chronic backache is obviously the most easily treated. You need to use proper body mechanics so as not to irritate your back during sex. We must warn you against falling into an enduring sex-avoidance pattern as a side-effect of backache; our habits have a way of sticking with us.

Most of us want to please and be pleased by our lovers. When sex is very painful because of a back condition, several kinds of emotional turmoil eventually affect both the partners. Without clear communication, misunderstandings quickly build up. For example, the pain-free partner may become less physically affectionate out of consideration for the lover's backache. However, the disabled mate may interpret this as rejection, punishment or loss of love. The disabled person may then react with guilt, depression or hostility which in turn may provoke rejection or counter-hospitality on the part of the 'considerate' non-disabled lover. A vicious cycle, thus, starts, which candid conversation could have avoided from the beginning.

Then there is the situation in which a pre-existing sexual problem is worsened or revived by backache.

Again, medicines taken for pain-relief may decrease libido. Tranquilizers, sedatives and narcotic analgesics, all may reduce sexual drive. Corticosterioids may decrease the response to genital stimulation. These drugs may also induce impotence in males.

Let us now lay down a general plan for a more satisfying sex life for the backache sufferer and his/her lover.

Step 1 : Begin with the doctrine that if you had it good previously, you can have it just as good again. So start with a positive attitude : "I know it is a challenge, but after reading this I am going to make it better."

Step 2 : Talk to your lover. Try to discuss the problem in a warm, frank relaxed, compassionate manner. This is a direct approach. If you feel awkward or want to be subtle, place a bookmark on this page and leave the book where you lover just can't miss it.

This advice is most important. You must start communicating immediately...... just now !

Step 3 : You and your lover must approach the problem with a sincere attitude of co-operation setting the goal of most pleasure and least pain.

Step 4 : Expand your attitudes as well as your mind and heart. Non-coital sexual activities can be mutually gratifying experiences of love. Such methods include masturbation, fellatio and cunnilingus.

Step 5 : Thoroughly understand and follow the body-positions which are known to be pain-free while making love. The material presented here is based on the best contemporary clinical and scientific knowledge of the spine.

Step 6 : Devote a good amount of time to pre-coital preparation. You may need a warm-up period similar to that by athletes. Application of moist heat to the lower spine may help. Warm baths, showers or compresses help to limber up joints prior to having sexual relations. Many doctors encourage backache and arthritis patients to use such procedures as a part of foreplay. When a couple bathes together before sex, they get a mutual application of moist heat. The pleasure of such an experience often enables the forgetting of the therapeutic aspect of bathing.

Alternatively, the pain-free partner may stimulate specific pain-relieving points of Acupressure on his/her partner's body as a part of the foreplay.

How to make love with a back problem :

(1) Do not bend forward with the knees straight, even if you are lying down, as this position puts tremendous strain on the lower spine. It also stretches the sciatic nerve, possibly irritating it. Bending the spine slightly forward is okay only if you bend your knees.

(2) Try to maintain correct pelvic tilt (i.e., avoid hollowing of the low back) during the intercourse. Arching the back makes the disc bulge toward the back and places much stress on the posterior structures of the spine, such as, the facet joints.

(3) Stay away from positions – like lying flat on your stomach or back with your hips extended straight – that stretch, stress or load the psoas muscles running from the front of the lumbar spine to just below the hip joint. When you flex (bend) one or both hips, you relax those muscles and take pressure off your lower back, protecting it.

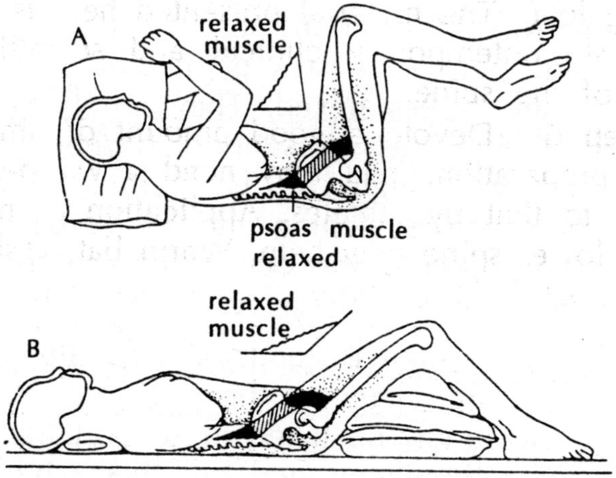

Fig. 10.1

Shown below are some body-positions during an intercourse that are good and safe for a backache victim. Figures 10.2 to 10.6 are especially good for female patients; all positions are good for male patients. The drawings should speak for themselves, but the captions include some commentary which you should review carefully.

You can invent your own, ingenious positions, as long as both of you remain pain-free. Remember, some of mankind's greatest discoveries have come from trial and error.

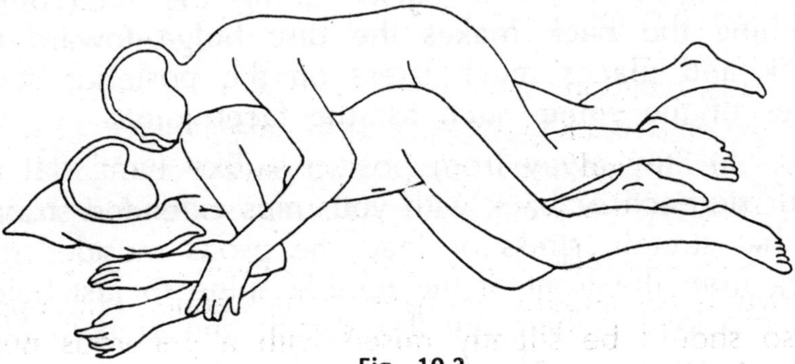

Fig. 10.2

This is the basic first line of defence basic to the "loving backache" position. It's the best for the female or the male with back pain. Both partners have their hips and knees flexed. They are lying on their sides so neither has to support his/her own body weight nor the weight of the partner. The female should guard against getting into a swayback position here. This position is the one of choice if you want to make love in a fairly acute stage of backache.

The next position is good for a female with backache. It takes advantage of the principle described in Fig. 10.1 Care must be taken to support the woman's upper torso with pillows and her thighs by the male lover's thighs and arms.

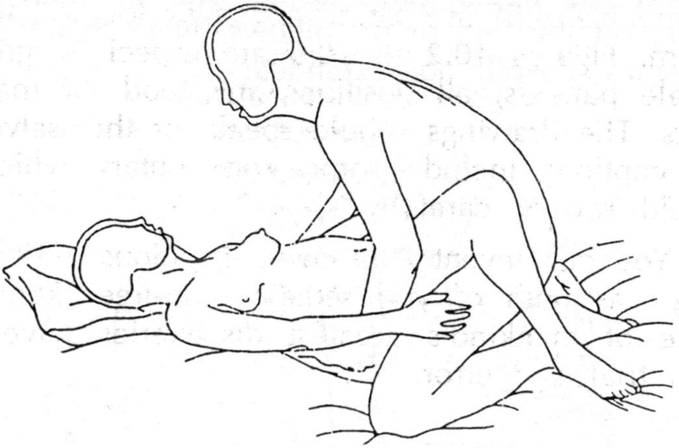

Fig. 10.3

The position shown in Fig. 10.4 is good for a female with back pain. Like the male in Fig. 10.3 her hips are flexed, she can avoid swayback, and she can support the weight the upper torso on her hands.

This can also be a good position for the male shown here, should he have a backache. The upper torso should be slightly raised with a generous number of pillows so as to flex the spine slightly and you must not be vigorous here.

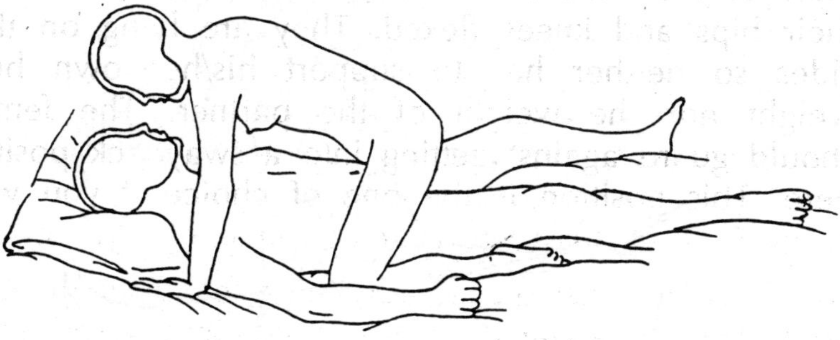

Fig. 10.4

The position we find the male in Fig. 10.5 may be good for the male with back pain. The reason is that the hips are flexed and the male can and should support his upper torso using one or both hands resting on the bed or on pillows. Note that his back is slightly flexed, not extended.

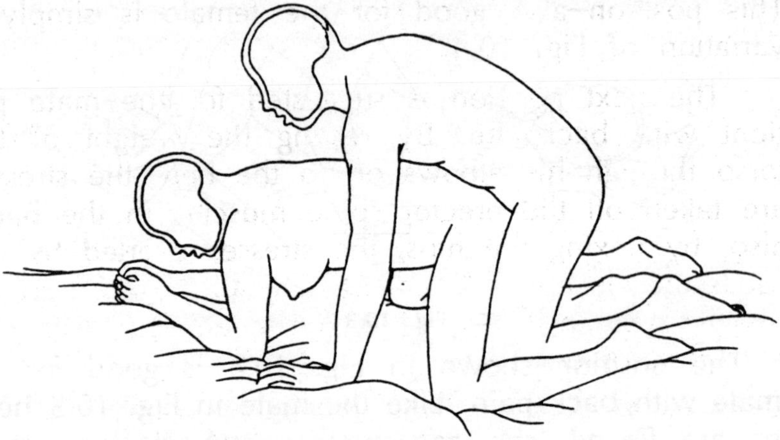

Fig. 10.5

A woman using this position may aggravate back pain if she is vigorously active, or, if her lover puts too much weight on her. A variation that will help the woman with backache is to have both partners with their knees on the floor with the female's upper torso fully supported by a bed, couch or chair.

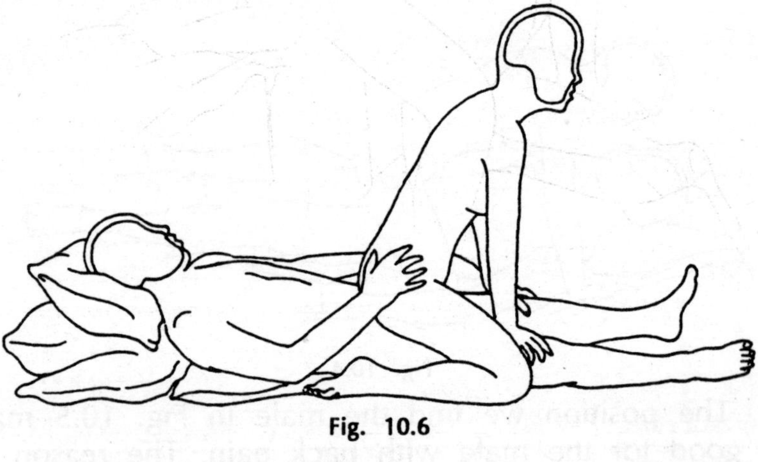

Fig. 10.6

Remember that if this position, which is good for the male with backache is to be used, pressure on the man's knees from the woman's hands may irritate his back by stimulating activity in the psoas muscle. This position—also good for the female—is simply a variation of Fig. 10.4.

The next position is suggested for the male patient with backache. By resting the weight of the torso through his elbows on to the bed, the stresses are taken off the erector spine muscles in the back; also, by flexing the hips, the stresses exerted by the psoas muscle are reduced. Of course, the position we see the woman in here is not for a female lover with a back problem.

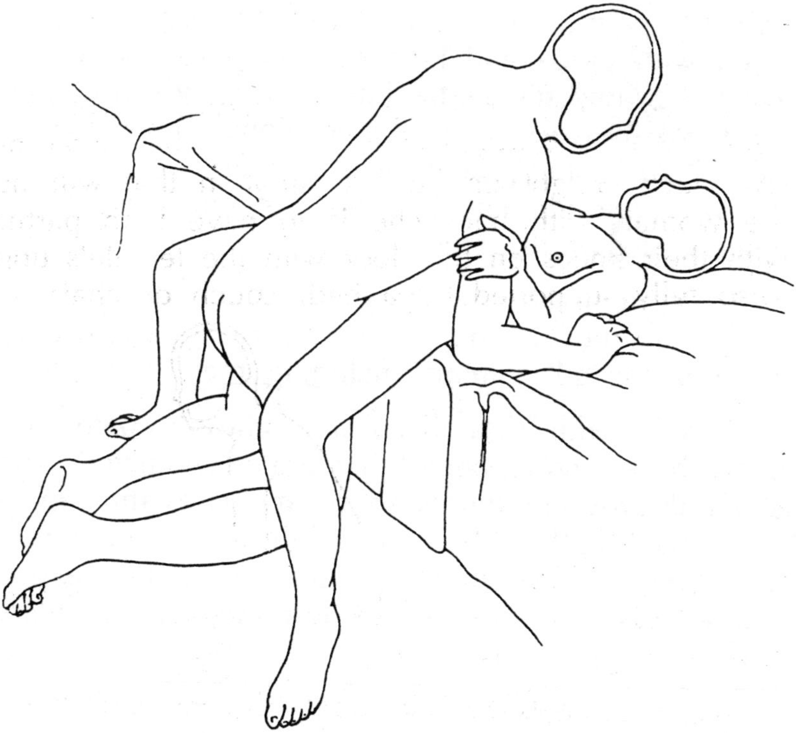

Fig. 10.7

When to resume love-making?

You may have had to abstain from intercourse for a few days because of backache. When is it safe to resume this natural activity? First, some negative prescriptions : Not when you have severe pain : Not the very first day or night you go off the medications.

When you can walk without much pain and require little or nothing in the way of pain-killers, try a practice run. We refer to this as making love with air, as you slowly try sexual manoeuvres without your partner. If there is no pain, try it again a little more vigorously. If there is no pain again, try a dry run (still with air) in one or two of the recommended positions. If you develop a sore back, wait for a day or two before resuming your affair with air. If you have no pain, break off the relationship with air (albeit with grace and kindness, as you may have to revive it). Now try gentle intercourse with your lover in one of the recommended positions. Once you can make love without pain or the pain is much less than the pleasure and does not last more than a few minutes afterwards, enjoy !

In conclusion, we may say that sexual intercourse is one of the most rewarding and natural activities for all animals including man.

People with disabilities and chronic pain commonly have sexual needs that are accentuated. Their sexual desires are increased by the constant need to be reassured that their disabilities do not repulse their loved ones. However, they may not express their excessive desire for sex lest they be considered unusual or perverse.

Some patients, despite their accentuated mental desires, may refrain from sex, afraid of worsening their back problem or incurring pain. However, if correct body-positions are adopted, there is little to worry about. In fact, patients suffering from chronic pain have indicated during surveys, that sexual activity made them feel better. Some even said that the sexual act relieved their pain. A number of studies, too, have given testimony to this fact. It may well be that the pain is still there, but after a positive sexual experience, it stops bothering the person quite so much.

Unfortunately, some readers may want to disregard the advice given in this chapter. Such will be the case of those who use backache as a means to avoid intimacy and sex. The statement, "Not tonight dear, I have a backache," has meaningful connotations. In a lighter vein, it has been said that, backache is world's best contraceptive !

11. ANSWERS TO SOME QUESTIONS PATIENTS COMMONLY ASK

Note : We have included such important questions in this chapter, the answers to which do not figure in the earlier chapters.

Q. 1. I have heard that most pregnant women suffer from backaches. My husband wants a baby but I am quite scared. What should I do ?

Ans. It is true that pregnant women are more susceptible to back pain. The reason for this is quite obvious. Picture a woman five months pregnant. The forward load she is carrying in her abdomen has accentuated the hollow of her back. This, along with the laxity of her abdominal muscles, makes her back muscles to overwork producing their fatigue. If these muscles were weak before pregnancy, the additional strain (workload) placed on them will give rise to pain.

At this point let us quickly reassure any woman who might be considering a future pregnancy with alarm in view of the possibilities of backache. There is absolutely no need to endure backache during pregnancy. In a number of industries, workers have to lift heavy weights and carry them through considerable distances during the entire day. Yet they don't suffer from backaches. That is because of the strength and flexibility of muscles associated with the back. Proper conditioning exercises before pregnancy (and during also, but only under the advice of your gynecologist) will enable you to sail through the nine months of pregnancy with no back problems whatsoever.

Exercises are essential after pregnancy to recondition the lengthened abdominal muscles. This is an especially vulnerable period for a woman's back since it will be subjected to heavy stress by her bending, lifting and carrying the baby day in and day out. Correct exercises at this time will go a long way to prevent a lifetime of chronic backache.

When there is an incompatibility between the demands placed on your spine and its capability to withstand them, it makes no difference whether you are man or a woman; the result for both sexes is a backache. Indeed, men with pot bellies are as susceptible to backache as are pregnant women !

Q. 2. A doctor has told me my pain is all in my head. I am terribly upset. What do you suggest ?

Ans. Psychiatrists and psychologists have been telling doctors again and again never to tell a patient that the pain is all in his / her head (i.e., the patient is imagining the pain), since that tends to make the patient angry and unco-operative. When a person is told his pain is imaginary he may go about, consciously or unconsciously, trying to prove it is real. This makes the pain more deeply embedded and subsequently harder to dislodge.

There is a difference between having the pain strictly in your head and having your backache affected by what is going on in your head. Unfavourable circumstances at your home, at your office or, in general, in your life can certainly cause or aggravate a backache.

If a doctor inadvertently tells you your pain is psychological, don't get upset. Realize that emotional problems that result out of stressful times, are every bit as painful as a broken leg. Try to co-operate with your doctor, as ninety-nine times out of hundred, he or she is truly interested in helping you.

Q. 3. I have been told by two eminent orthopaedists that I will have to live with my pain. Is there no way out for me ?

Ans. We wish we could guarantee all our patients a life free from back pain. But occasionally such a wish does not materialise. As we have said earlier, almost 90 per cent of backaches are due to a spasm of back muscles. Such backaches, sooner or later, go away. However, if your backache is not because of muscle spasm but due to some other cause, especially a disease, its course will depend upon the course of that disease. If that disease runs a prolonged or indefinitely course, your backache, too, will linger on indefinitely. You may, then, have to learn to live with it. However, you may be able to substantially reduce the discomfort by reconditioning your back (through exercises) and by following the tips mentioned below :

(1) Plan ahead at work.

(2) Change or modify the nature of your work so that you don't have to lift things.

(3) Make sure your chair is comfortable and gives good support to your spine.

(4) When you have been sitting for an hour or so, get up and move around. Don't allow the pain to render you physically inactive.

(5) If you have to change a job, do so earlier rather than later, i.e. while you are young enough to re-train.

(6) Plan ahead at home, too.

(7) Remember that housework isn't as important as your back. Don't allow the housework to unduly tire you and your spine.

(8) If you have small children, lift them as little as possible.

(9) See if there are any mechanical devices that can make life easier for you.

(10) Finally, and this is very important, keep your spirit up. Spontaneous recovery, even from a so-called 'incurable' disease, is not an impossibility. Indeed, a number of such cases have been recorded. Norman Cousins, a renowned writer, was able to

defeat 'ankylosing spondylitis' with positive mental attitude and laughter. We wholeheartedly recommend his interesting and inspiring book 'Anatomy of an Illness' to all interested readers.*

Q. 4. Recently I have heard of a new treatment for pain-relief called TENS. What is TENS ? What is its place in the treatment of backache ? Does it compare favourably with Acupressure or Acupuncture ?

Ans. The letters TENS stand for trans-cutaneous electrical nerve stimulation. It, undoubtedly, produces noticeable pain-relief. The mechanism for pain-relief is, perhaps, similar to that which follows Acupressure treatment.

A study (E. S. Fox and R. Melzack, Pain, 2:114, 1976) comparing the two methods of treatment shows a significant amount of pain-reduction with both techniques. The reduction of pain was achieved in 75 per cent of patients treated with Acupuncture and slightly less number (66 per cent) of patients with TENS. However, those treated with Acupuncture enjoyed somewhat prolonged pain-relief (for 40 hours) as compared to that with TENS (for 23 hours).

We will say that Acupressure is somewhat preferable because (a) it is inexpensive, (b) it is a form of self-treatment and (c) its efficacy in relieving back-pain has been proved by numerous clinical trials.

Q. 5. What is subluxation ? What is chiropractic subluxation ?

Ans. Subluxation can be defined as partial dislocation or displacement of a vertebra with respect to other adjacent vertebra/e.

---

* The authors have adapted this book into Gujarati, naming it 'Man Jaage Toe Rog Bhaage (મન જાગે તો રોગ ભાગે)'

The subluxation that chiropractors refer to has not been seen by independent observers.

In chiropractic manipulation, the subluxated vertebrae are supposedly manipulated back into their normal position. The chiropractic hypothesis is that as a vertebra slips out again, you have pain and it must be put back once more. This process can go on ad infinitum, and manipulations are sometimes sold in prepaid packages, each of a certain number of treatments.

If a vertebra is pushed back into place, why assume it would stay there ? And why would continually pushing it back ever make it stick ? These are some questions which have no answers

Q. 6. I have heard of a new type of surgery in which the herniated disc is removed through a little, thin tube inserted into the spine. Won't that be safer than the usual 'laminectomy', which necessitates the opening up of the back ?

Ans. There is no doubt that this procedure involves less surgery than the usual laminectomy for disc excision. The question is whether the benefits of that reduction in surgery outweigh the limitations of the procedure.

If a person has a very specific kind of disc problem, where there is a clear-cut displacement of a disc that is lying in just the right place so that the nerves can be moved out of the way and the disc can be easily removed, then the plus points of this procedure do outweigh its minus points.

On the other hand, if a disc is not displaced in a particular way, the procedure may be able to remove only a part of that disc, or none at all.

In short, there are numerous factors that compromise or limit the efficacy of this method.

Q. 7. What is a myelogram ?

Ans. Myelogram literally means a radiograph (X-ray picture) of the spinal canal.

In myelography, a special dye (called the contrast medium) is injected into the 'subarachnoid space' around the spinal cord and the nerves. The contrast medium shows up on the radiograph as a dense white image. If something (e.g., a herniated disc) is pressing upon a spinal nerve-root, it looks like an indentation in the column of dye.

Thus, myelography is a special investigative procedure that is undertaken before contemplating any disc surgery.

Myelography is usually a painful procedure carrying some risks, especially those of production of allergy to the dye used.

Q. 8. What is an EMG study ?

Ans. The letters EMG stand for electromyography, an investigative procedure undertaken to determine if a herniated disc is causing nerve-root irritation.

In this test, very fine needles are inserted into selected muscles. The electrical impulses generated in these muscles are taken up by the inserted needles and the nature of these impulses recorded. Irritation of a spinal nerve-root shows up as abnormal electrical responses.

Q. 9. What is a CAT scan ? Can it diagnose a herniated disc ?

Ans. The letters CAT stand for computerized axial tomography. A CAT scan is a new development in diagnostic radiology. Through sophisticated imaging, it can 'photograph' the spine clearly in several cross sections.

Depending on the technological capabilities of the scanner (machine) used, a CAT scan can rather reliably reveal a herniated disc. Soon, the CAT scan may supplant the myelogram in many circumstances.

It is almost painless and since usually no dye is injected into the spine, the question of allergy does not arise.

Q. 10. Should a person who has undergone back-surgery perform exercises ?

Ans. Graded exercises, done under the direction of a surgeon, should form an integral part of post-surgical back-care. Muscle atrophy, stiffness and weakness are common after-effects of surgery. A careful exercise regime can check such undesirable after-effects.

In fact, if the back muscles are reconditioned with appropriate exercises, the need for a possible second or third operation might be averted.

APPENDIX 1

ACUPRESSURE

Acupressure is an oriental therapy which strives to treat disorders by stimulating specific points lying on the skin, with finger or thumb-pressure. In Acupuncture, the same points are stimulated by inserting needles into them.

Both Acupressure and Acupuncture are used throughout the world, especially to relieve pain. They are official modes of treatment in the hospitals of Oriental countries like China, Korea and Japan. The World Health Organisations (W.H.O.), too, recognizes them as authentic modes of treatment and recommends their use in a number of diseases a list of which was published in the Dec. '79 issue of the organization's magazine 'World Health'.

Without 'beating about the bush' any further, let us come to the practical part i.e., where are backache-relieving points located and how to stimulate them. Since Acupressure is new to you, you should expect an initial period of unfamiliarity and awkwardness. During this period, the results you obtain may be somewhat disappointing. This initial period is, in effect, the period of 'apprenticeship'. It is quite brief for most people. But we want to be sure you are prepared for it. Acupressure is a simple skill to master, but it is a skill none the less; it must be learned. Your confidence and the sureness of your fingers and thumbs will improve with practice. So will grow the efficacy of the technique in relieving pain and muscle-spasm. We make a point of this because we don't want you to give in to early disappointment.

Except by luck, you are not likely to find the points precisely or stimulate them in the right way the first time you try. When you do master the technique, however, you may find that the relief comes faster than is possible with medicines.

For satisfactory results, you should press the recommended points quite firmly. Therefore, you must use your nails. Pressing with the fleshy pads or bony tips of your thumbs may have little or no effect on the nerves you are attempting to stimulate because they lie quite deep beneath the skin.

Your thumb nails should be short and rounded so that you do not injure the skin while pressing a point. If the nails are kept trim and well-maintained, there will be no bruising or other injury to the skin.

How much pressure : Though this point has been covered in the earlier discussion, we will reiterate that you must press upon the indicated points hard enough to make them hurt briefly. As you will discover, some of them are exquisitely tender (painful). In fact, the feeling of tenderness will be a signal that you have hit the point with precision. Do not worry. The pain will not last long, and your reward for enduring it will be the alleviation of much longer-lasting pain in your back. Please understand once again that you must press hard; insufficient pressure will fail to produce the desired effect of pain-relief.

How long ? : Stimulate each point rythmically (press-release-press) for about a minute or a minute and a half.

When ? : The points should be stimulated once or twice a day (or as often as required). Unlike medicines, you just can't overdose yourself with Acupressure ! Most persons find that a single treatment keeps their backs pain-free for hours together.

Given below are diagrams and descriptions of useful points. See them, understand them, learn them. Then put your knowledge into action right away, for pain-relief without drugs–the Acupressure way!

Notes : (1) It is not necessary to stimulate points on both sides of the body, unless of course the feat can be accomplished without sparing special time (i.e., if the points on the right and the left side of the body can be stimulated simultaneously). Adequate pain-relief will be obtained even by pressing points of any one side of the body.

(2) Some Acupressure points are described as located at some particular distance from prominent parts of the body. But for measuring distances on the humam body, units like inches or centimetres are useless since no two persons have similar builds. The Chinese have invented an ingenious method to overcome the difficulty. To locate Acupressure points accurately, they use, what is called the 'body-inch' or 'thumb-inch'. The diagram given below is self-explanatory.

width of thumb = one thumb-inch

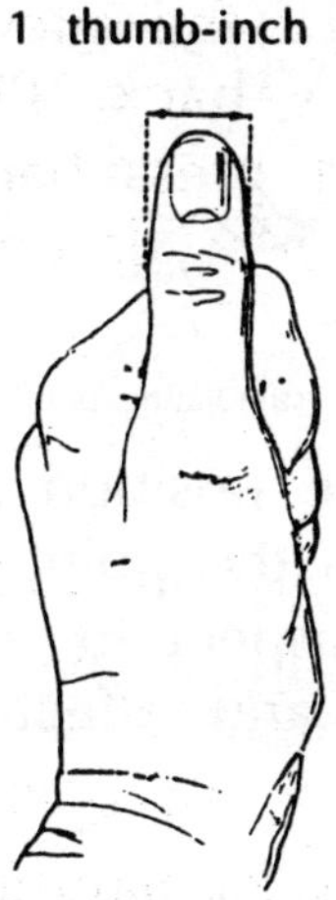

Point 1

Location : This useful point is located on the fleshy part between the thumb and the index finger, about one and a half thumb-inches from the web margin. The point is easy to locate on account of its tenderness (painfulness on pressure).

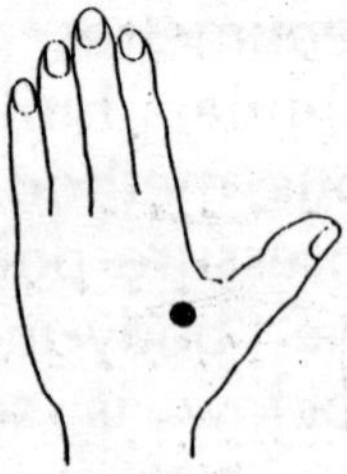

Point 1

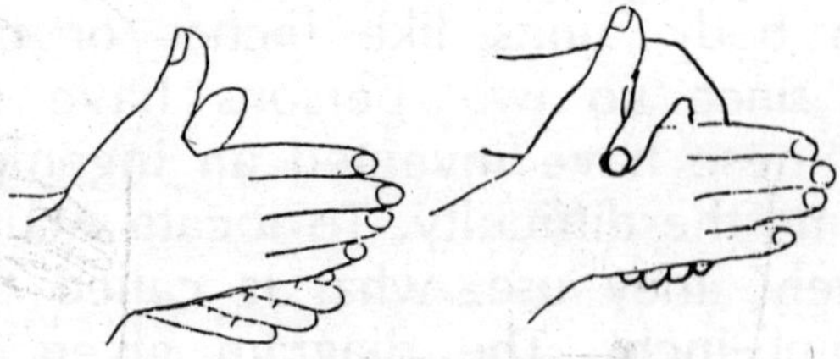

method of locations point 1

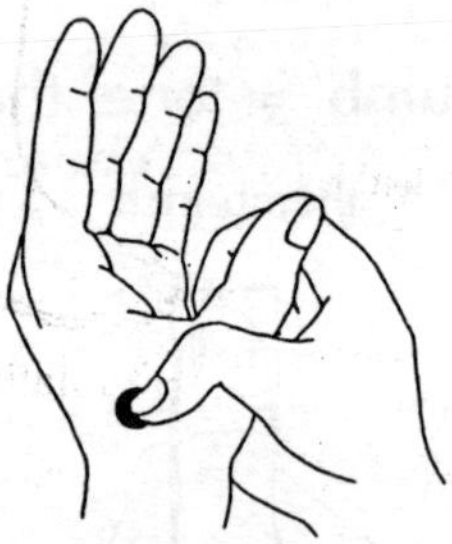

stimulating point 1

Stimulation : The position shown above, wherein the thumb-tip lies on the point and one of the fingers lies on the palmar aspect to provide firm apposition, is quite convenient and effective.

Point 2

Location : On the midpoint of the crease at the back of the knee.

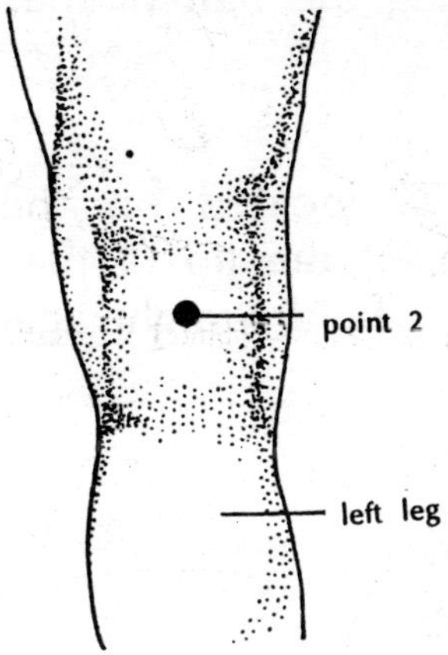

point 2

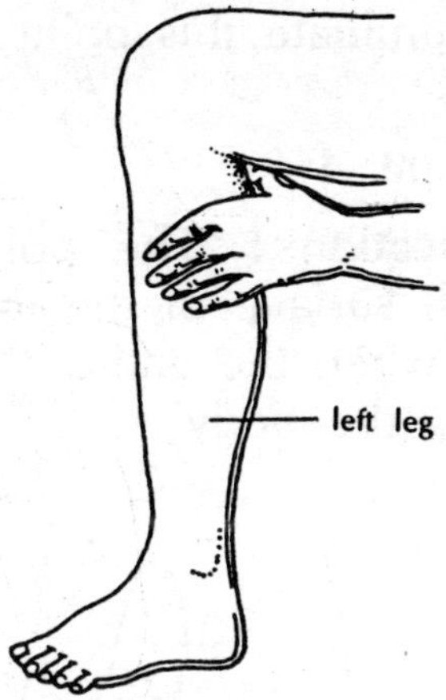

stimulating point 2

Stimulation : A convenient position of the hand for the stimulation of this point has been depicted on the figure given above.

Point 3

Location : On the midpoint of the crease below the buttock (i.e., the crease that demarcates the buttock from the thigh).

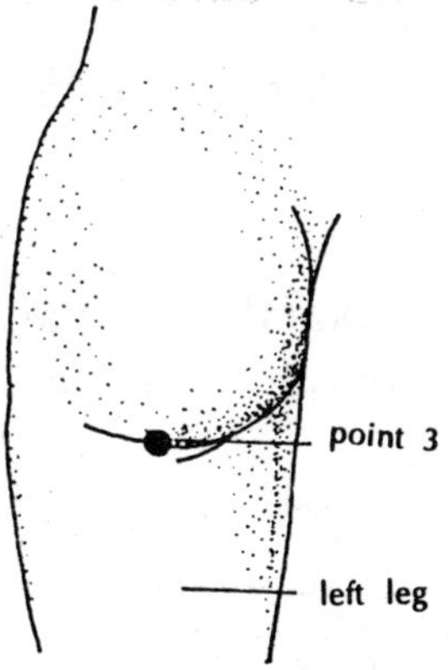

point 3

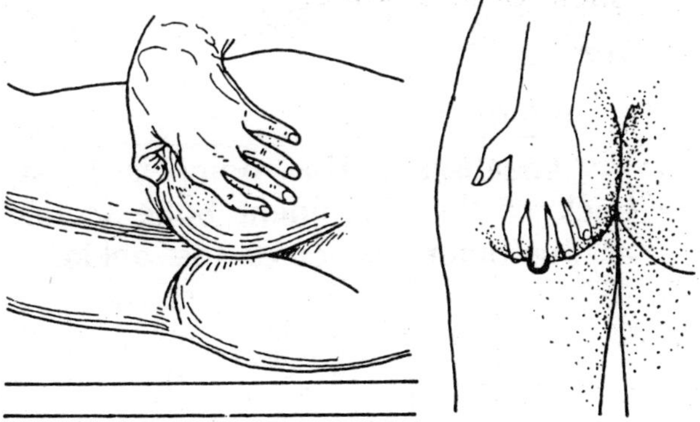

stimulating point 3

Stimulation : This point can be stimulated standing or lying down. Persons who have inflexible wrists may stimulate this point using the nail of the middle finger.

Point 4

Location : The point is located on the outer (lateral) surface of the thigh, at the tip of the middle finger when the entire arm is held straight against the side of the body.

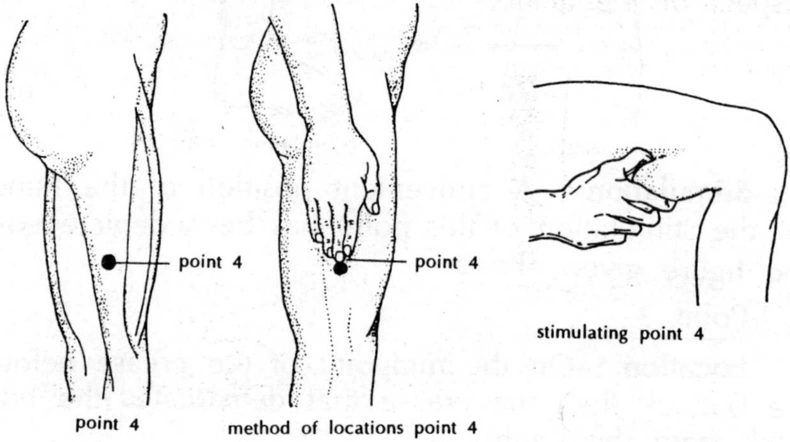

Stimulation : The point can be pressed bilaterally, in the sitting position. The fingers can be wrapped around the under-surface of the thighs for extra leverage.

Point 5

Location : This point is located exactly at the back of the prominent bone (called lateral maleolus) at the outer aspect of the ankle.

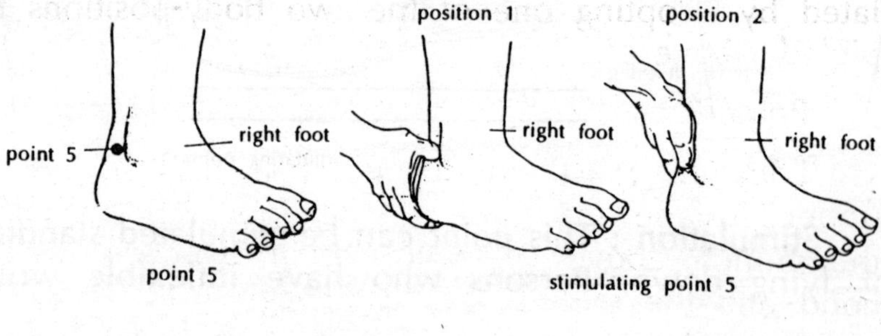

Stimulation : Two convenient positions of the hand, for the stimulation of this point have been depicted above.

Point 6

Location : This point is located exactly below the prominent bone (called lateral maleolus) at the outer aspect of the ankle.

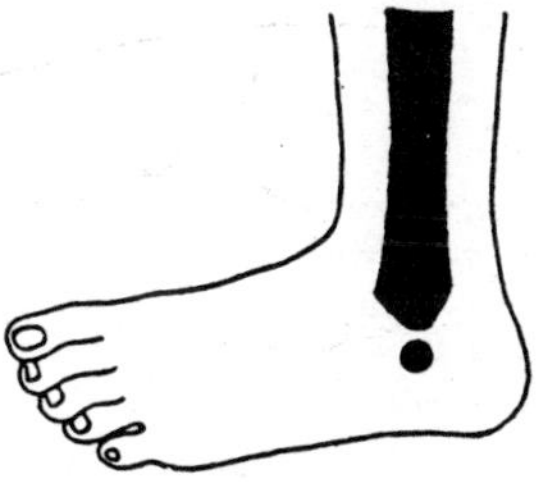

point 6

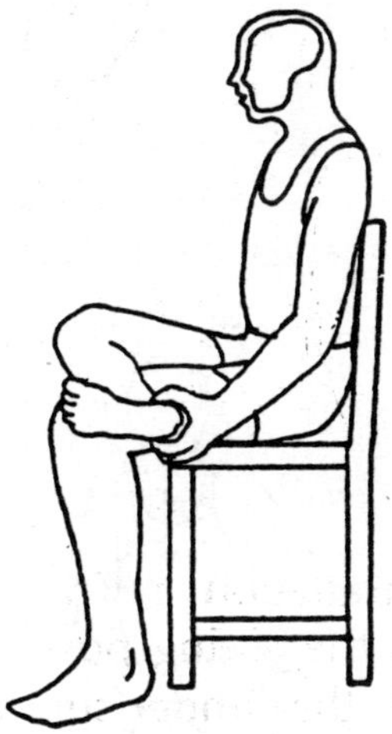

position 2

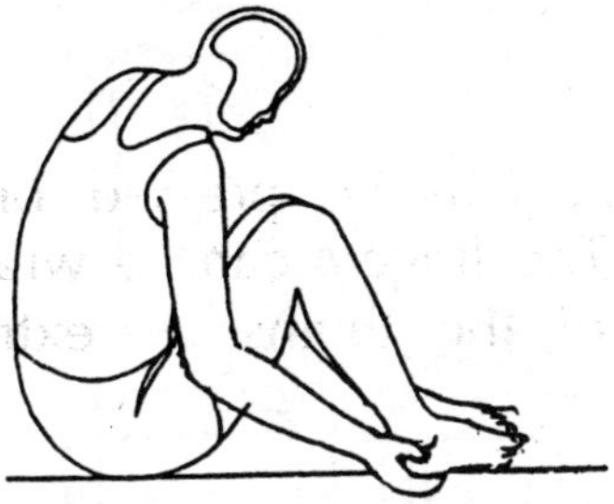

position 1

stimulating point 6

Stimulation : The point can be conveniently stimulated by adopting one of the two body-positions depicted above.

Point 7

Location : This useful point is located on the upper surface (dorsum) of the foot, about half a thumb-inch above the web-margin between the second and the middle toes (see page 188).

Stimulation : Two convenient positions to stimulate this point have been shown. Most persons find position 1 more suitable.

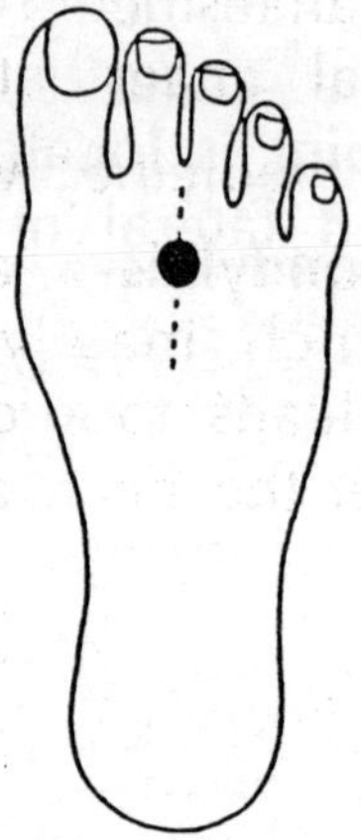

position 7

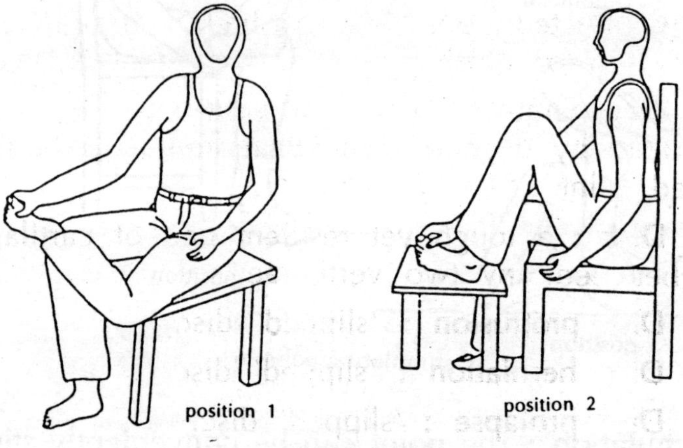

position 1

position 2

stimulating point 7

APPENDIX 2

GLOSSARY

(1) **Anaesthetic** : a medicine which causes unconsciousness (general anaesthetic) or suppresses pain if injected locally (local anaesthetic).

(2) **Analgesic** : a medicine which relieves pain.

(3) **Ankylosing spondylitis** : an arthritic disease of unknown cause which mainly affects young or middle-aged men and leads to progressive and painful stiffness of the spine, the neck and sometimes hips and shoulders.

(4) **Cervical** : pertaining to the neck.

(5) **Corticosteroids** : group of drugs which act like hormones and used to reduce inflammation.

(6) **Crush fracture** : sudden internal fracture in which the affected bone gets crushed; vertebrae are common sites for crush fractures.

(7) **Degenerative joint – disease** : a condition characterized by degeneration (wear and tear) of the concerned joint.

(8) **Disc** : a tough yet resilient pad of cartilage present between any two vertebrae.

(9) **Disc protrusion** : 'slipped' disc.

(10) **Disc herniation** : 'slipped' disc.

(11) **Disc prolapse** : 'slipped' disc.

(12) **Dislocation** : a displacement of the two bones that form a joint, so that all apposition is lost.

(13) **Dorsal (synonym - thoracic)** : pertaining to the upper and middle back.

(14) Fibrositis : aches and pains in and around muscles of the shoulder and shoulder blades.

(15) Foramen (pl - foramina) : a small hole or opening in a bone (e.g., in a vertebra, for transmission of the spinal nerve).

(16) Herniated disc : 'slipped' disc.

(17) Hydrocortisone : a natural hormone produced in the adrenal gland of the body; also available as a medicine (in oral drops or injection forms) to reduce inflammation.

(18) Inflammation : reaction of body-tissues to an injury or an infection, characterized by heat, swelling, redness and pain of the concerned part.

(19) Kyphosis : an exaggerated backward curvature of the spine, particularly in the upper back region.

(20) Lesion : injury or disease-change in organs and tissues.

(21) Ligament : short band of tough yet flexible tissue binding muscles and bones together.

(22) Lordosis : an exaggerated forward curvature of the spine, particularly in the lower back region.

(23) Lumbago : backache.

(24) Lumbar : pertaining to the lower back.

(25) Malignant : cancerous (when applied to tumours).

(26) Manipulation : a manual procedure consisting of pulling, pushing, turning or twisting body-parts with a view to restoring correct alignment.

(27) Neuritis : inflammation of one or more nerves.

(28) Osteomalacia : a disease of adults caused by deficiency of vitamin D in diet and lack of sunshine; it is characterized by softness of bones.

(29) Osteoporosis : an abnormal decrease in the density of bones rendering them porous and brittle.

(30) Paget's disease : a disorder in which bones of the spine, legs or the skull become patchily thickened, leading to bending of long bones and enlargement of the skull.

(31) Periosteum : the thin membrane around bones.

(32) Prolapsed disc : 'slipped' disc.

(33) Rheumatism : a non-specific term, embracing a diverse group of diseases which have, in common, disorder or disease of connective tissue and hence, usually present with pain or stiffness or swelling of joints and muscles.

(34) Rheumatoid arthritis : a chronic, progressive and inflammatory disease affecting many joints simultaneously and causing pain, swelling and stiffness.

(35) Rickets : a disorder of children due to a deficiency of vitamin D and/or too little sunshine, characterized by softness of bones.

(36) Sacrum : a triangular bone at the lower end of the spine, formed by the fusion of five sacral vertebrae; it gives attachment to the hip bones.

(37) Sciatica : pain running down the thigh and the leg due to inflammation or irritation of, or pressure on, the sciatic nerve.

(38) Scoliosis : an abnormal sideward bending of the spine.

(39) Sedative : a medicine which soothes and calms the nerves and the mind.

(40) Slipped disc : a disc which has partially moved out of place.

(41) Spinal osteoarthritis : a gradual degeneration of the spine (especially of the neck and the lower back region).

(42) Spondylolisthesis : slipping forward of one vertebra on another.

(43) Spondylosis : degenerative changes in the spine.

(44) Spondylitis : inflammation of the joints of the spine.

(45) Subluxation : incomplete dislocation of a joint.

(46) Tendon : strong band of tissue which attaches the fleshy part of muscle to a bone.

(47) Traction : a physical treatment consisting of pulling the spine along its axis (length), with a view to decompressing spinal nerve/s.

(48) Vertebra : a bone of the vertebral column.

(49) Vertebral column : a column of small bones (vertebrae) that are placed one above the other and joined together with ligaments and discs to form the spine.